NEW DIRECTIONS FOR INSTITUTIONAL RESEARCH

J. Fredericks Volkwein, Per
EDITOR-IN-CHIEF

D0870891

Higher Education as Competitive Enterprise:
When Markets Matter

Robert Zemsky,
University of Pennsylvania

Susan Shaman
University of Pennsylvania

Daniel B. Shapiro
University of Pennsylvania

AUTHORS

Number 111, Fall 2001

 JOSSEY-BASS
A Wiley Company
989 Market Street
San Francisco, CA 94103-1741

HIGHER EDUCATION AS COMPETITIVE ENTERPRISE: WHEN MARKETS MATTER
Robert Zemsky, Susan Shaman, Daniel B. Shapiro (aus.)
New Directions for Institutional Research, no. 111
Volume XXIX, Number 3
J. Fredericks Volkwein, Editor-in-Chief

New Directions for Institutional Research is indexed in *College Student Personnel Abstracts, Contents Pages in Education,* and *Current Index to Journals in Education* (ERIC).

Microfilm copies of issues and chapters are available in 16mm and 35mm, as well as microfiche in 105mm, through University Microfilms Inc., 300 North Zeeb Road, Ann Arbor, Michigan 48106–1346.

ISSN 0271-0579   ISBN 0-7879-5795-X

NEW DIRECTIONS FOR INSTITUTIONAL RESEARCH is part of The Jossey-Bass Higher and Adult Education Series and is published quarterly by Jossey-Bass, 989 Market Street, San Francisco, California 94103-1741 (publication number USPS 098-830). Periodicals postage paid at San Francisco, California, and at additional mailing offices. POSTMASTER: Send address changes to New Directions for Institutional Research, Jossey-Bass, 989 Market Street, San Francisco, California 94103-1741.

SUBSCRIPTIONS cost $59.00 for individuals and $109.00 for institutions, agencies, and libraries.

EDITORIAL CORRESPONDENCE should be sent to J. Fredericks Volkwein, Center for the Study of Higher Education, Penn State University, 400 Rackley Building, University Park, PA 16801-5252.

Photograph of the library by Michael Graves at San Juan Capistrano by Chad Slattery © 1984. All rights reserved.

www.josseybass.com

Printed in the United States of America on acid-free recycled paper containing 100 percent recovered waste paper, of which at least 20 percent is postconsumer waste.

For Martin Meyerson, who first asked the questions it took us twenty years to answer.

CONTENTS

AUTHORS' NOTES

Antecedents

Twenty years is a long time to pursue a research interest that itself was an accident of time and place. The University of Pennsylvania, like most high-price/high-cost colleges and universities in the mid-1970s, discovered it was likely to run out of students. Too few children had been born during the baby bust that had followed the baby boom, and too many of these students and their parents had packed up and moved to warmer climes. The challenge facing Penn was to determine how to get them back to Philadelphia, at least for their college years. The university's charge to us was to assess the changing demographics so that a rejuvenated admissions office could go "hunting where the ducks were." What was needed, we concluded, was a model that estimated the likely possibility that students in a given area outside of the Northeast would consider matriculating at an institution like Penn.

We now know, although frankly did not appreciate then, that the key to solving the admissions puzzle was a broad understanding of the market for postsecondary education: what higher education's customers were looking for and how they were likely to respond to specific educational offerings; what institutions had to do to better serve the market; and how institutions could stay true to their missions even as they became increasingly sophisticated and disciplined in both their messages and their operations.

We also learned that higher education's market awareness evolved in unexpected ways. Admissions officers were often the first to talk about markets—although had one asked them, they would have likely said that their interests lay more with recruiting plans than market strategies and that their use of market terms was more metaphorical than technical. At the same time much of the academic research focusing on higher education proved to be wide of the mark. It tended to look at colleges and universities as institutions rather than enterprises and was more likely to take at face value what institutions and institutional leaders said about costs and prices or about student and institutional needs. However sophisticated their analysis of other kinds of institutions and contexts, most academics described their own environments as being too complex, and therefore researchers found it too difficult—if not actually impossible—to develop reliable measures of quality and effectiveness in higher education.

All has now changed. People talk about markets, whether or not they understand them. Most people are also uncomfortable with what they see, or think they see: students using the power of their purchases to define what they need to learn, faculty and departments overly sensitive to things that sell as opposed to ideas that matter, and administrations adopting the policies and practices of businesses in order to make a quintessentially messy endeavor more efficient. Everywhere the byword is *competition*—competition for students, for faculty, for research dollars, for donors, and perhaps the unkindest cut of all, for a better score in the dreaded collegiate rankings. The market now matters in higher education.

Our own work over these last twenty years has both served as an accelerator of and been shaped by these trends. At times we prematurely celebrated the power of markets to remake higher education. Other times we underestimated the difficulties inherent in making institutions market smart. Yet we believe we have been consistent in our quest for a set of working definitions and tools that can make the machinations of the market both more understandable and more rational. We have put forth measures and models that allow institutions to better play the "what if" game. We have explored the role language can play in making the inevitable intriguing. We have also sought to understand how the special nature of higher education bends and recasts the basic disciplines of the market—as well as when, where, and how colleges and universities represent economic enterprises that are subject to the same rules and constraints that shape the behavior of other businesses in a market economy.

Inklings

Our first step in pursuing Penn's charge, and in examining the vicissitudes of the market, was to build an enrollment planning model, having persuaded the College Board that its data held the key for allowing not just Penn but all institutions to chart their likely admissions futures. The eventual products were two: the College Board's Enrollment Planning Service (EPS) and a monograph focusing on what we had come to call *The Structure of College Choice* (Zemsky and Oedel, 1983). We mapped the college admissions market in terms of its national, regional, in-state, and local segments. Moreover, we demonstrated just how deeply those seams were etched into the social fabric of the nation—that unfortunately, it took painfully few socioeconomic attributes to predict the kind of institutions to which high school seniors were likely to apply. Knowing where the ducks were, it turned out, was really a matter of knowing which kinds of ducks one was hunting.

We transformed this initial, but somewhat limited, interest in the workings of the college admissions process into a focus on markets rather than demographics via an invitation from Larry Litten. For a new volume in the Jossey-Bass series New Directions for Institutional Research, Litten came looking for a fresh and clever way of talking about tuition levels and their impact on the range of college choice.

As is so often the case in our work together, we began by talking—in this case, taking on in our imaginations those college presidents who were increasingly likely to explain away escalating prices by comparing the cost of college to that of a new car. What would happen, we asked ourselves in mock horror, if colleges and universities were indeed priced like new cars?

The result was an essay that detailed in appropriately stark terms just how close the pricing of a college education had come to resemble the pricing of a new automobile. In each case one began with the sticker price, that is, the price at which the product was advertised and at times even sold. Then there was the discount price, what the seller actually expected to receive from the customer. For the new car it was the sticker price minus a trade-in and any additional reductions the buyer had managed to extract through bargaining. For a college education it was the "admissions catalog price" minus financial aid. Finally, there was the cash price—what the buyer actually paid in terms of constant dollars, having taken advantage of the seller's willingness to help finance the purchase through an advantageous loan package (Shaman and Zemsky, 1984).

Even then we thought we were simply writing about the college admissions market. Although we played easily with the notions of markets and prices, we never really extended the insight, never drew the now-obvious conclusion that higher education was indeed an enterprise—nay, an industry—that was increasingly being shaped by what would come to be recognized as market forces. As with the case of our work for the College Board, we thought little about the impact of this market's growing competitiveness for paying students on the nature or structure of the institutions that had willy-nilly become sellers as well as providers.

Although most of our work is rightly identified with the Institute for Research on Higher Education (IRHE), the work on enrollments and the admissions market commenced under the auspices of Penn's Office of Planning Analysis. The office's other large task in those years was to provide analytic support and conceptual underpinnings for the development of Penn's Responsibility Center Management (RCM) system. Conceived in the 1970s by John Hobstetter and made operational by Jon Straus, RCM made Penn's individual schools responsible for their revenues as well as their expenses—what they could spend was fundamentally limited by what they could earn, as supplemented by a university subvention. Although RCM was originally justified as a way to control expenses at a time when most people thought the university's budgets needed to shrink, most deans came to understand that the real challenge lay in encouraging their faculties' entrepreneurial behavior. Despite all of the tough talk about controlling expenses and the tough decisions about closing undersubscribed programs, it proved easier for faculty to sell rather than to discipline their aspirations.

Much of our work across the 1980s and into the 1990s represented an attempt to understand the economic incentives embedded in budget systems like RCM, systems that were being adopted by higher education institutions of nearly every stripe. Working with William Massy of Stanford University, we helped build the vocabulary that institutions as well as their critics used to make sense of changing economic circumstances. Some of the terms we introduced into these debates—particularly "the lattice and the ratchet"—provided a convenient shorthand that captured the frustration engendered by higher education's seeming inability to control expenses (*Policy Perspectives*, 1990). Our notion of institutions' core and perimeter functions (with the latter too often mislabeled as peripheral activities) provided a similar framework for explaining the heightened tension between higher education's traditionalists and its entrepreneurs (Zemsky, Massy, and Oedel, 1993). Unwittingly, we were well on our way to discovering the contours of the market.

Serendipity

Largely forgotten, by us as well as others, was our earlier work on the structure of the admissions market—forgotten until the competition for the U.S. Department of Education's Improving Postsecondary Education Research and Development Center returned us to where we had begun. The first imperative governing most competitions under the National Educational Research and Development Center Program is the need to respond to the request for a proposal (RFP) by promising to deliver what the Department of Education says it wants.

A remarkably short RFP governed the 1995 competition for the department's proposed center focusing on postsecondary education—less than one printed page listing the six priorities the winning bidder was expected to address. Among them was a somewhat cryptic call for research focusing on the "relationships among students' participation and progress in postsecondary education, their academic achievement, and their later employment outcomes." It was as though the committee responsible for drafting the RFP had been unable to decide which was more important, learning or labor market outcomes, and had simply decided the issue by concatenation. The Penn component of the Stanford–Penn–University of Michigan consortium that would win the competition drafted the research strategy and proposal for this priority.

We proposed that the only way to assess both learning and labor market outcomes was to look at how a sample of recent graduates actually turned out. Having helped win the competition that led to the establishment of the National Center for Postsecondary Improvement (NCPI), we then set about implementing our proposed study of higher education outcomes.

As we began, however, we discovered that none of the standard ways of classifying colleges and universities—not size, not control, not Carnegie classification, not national rankings—provided much help in explaining the kinds of outcomes we were extrapolating from available national data sets. Our stated task was to develop a new instrument leading to a new national data set that mapped both learning and labor market outcomes. To be useful to either institutions or their would-be students, however, the resulting analysis needed to group institutions as well as students into useful clusters. Thus a key part of the design process preceding the development of the instrument involved anticipating what those clusters might look like.

Then the nickel dropped. What would happen if we developed a clustering scheme that actually derived from the structure of the market for undergraduate institutions? Why not build that cluster system—a taxonomy, really—using what we knew about markets and how they worked, not just for higher education but for other high-priced goods and services as well? The resulting market taxonomy would need to meet two conditions. It would first have to explain the range of prices that different kinds of institutions charged. Second, it would have to demonstrate that the market's student shoppers were focusing their choices within, rather than across, market segments.

We presented our initial results in *Change* magazine in late 1997 (for four-year institutions) and in early 1998 (for two-year institutions). What we presented in *Change* was a pair of horizontal taxonomies, as opposed to a set of vertical rankings, that helped to explain a host of distributions important to higher education: from price to average faculty salaries to mean expenditures per full-time equivalent student to the utilization of part-time faculty to the ethnic distributions that had come to characterize U.S. higher education (Zemsky, Shaman, and Iannozzi, 1997; Institute for Research on Higher Education, 1998).

The appeal of our notion of a market taxonomy comprised of a set of market segments lay in its intuitive reasonableness. Although not everyone liked the specific cluster to which the taxonomy assigned their institutions, the ordered nature of the clustering as well as the taxonomy's operating terms made sense of the competitive environment that had come to dominate U.S. higher education. On *The Chronicle of Higher Education*'s back page, Chester Finn (1998, p. B4) celebrated what he called the functional virtues of thinking about markets instead of missions, opening his article with this observation:

> A quarter of a century after Clark Kerr and his colleagues devised an intricate classification system for U.S. colleges and universities, it's time to replace the Carnegie schema with one better attuned to today's realities.
>
> The old system sorted institutions into a dozen categories, ranging from "research" universities and "comprehensive" campuses to liberal arts and community colleges. The distinctions were based on academic mission rather than market niche. Now the National Center for Postsecondary Improvement . . . has devised a simple, three-part typology that I find clarifying and functional. It has already come to the attention of the commission chartered by Congress to study college costs, and I suspect that we will be hearing a great deal more about it in the days to come.

Refinements

From our perspective, however, the taxonomy's immediate importance remained in its ability to do what it was designed to do: help us make sense of the learning and labor market outcomes reflected in the National

Center for Education Statistics' key longitudinal surveys, High School and Beyond and the National Education Longitudinal Survey. That analysis provided much of the basis for the prototype of what we would come to call the Collegiate Results Instrument (CRI). We conducted the first test of the instrument during the winter of 1998 with samples of 1992 graduates drawn from fifteen institutions belonging to the Knight Higher Education Collaborative—in all, the 180 institutions then working with us on building a change agenda for higher education. The next year we tested a revised CRI using samples of graduates (drawn principally from the class of 1992–93) from eighty Knight Collaborative institutions. That test yielded just over thirty-eight thousand valid returns that have become the basis for our subsequent analysis of learning and labor market outcomes.

The CRI brought us back to the connection between market forces and educational outcomes—to our earlier insight that the market is a principal actor in the processes shaping colleges and universities. If markets were as important as we had come to argue, then those same markets should have a major role in determining the educational outcomes produced by groups of educational institutions. More had to be at stake than simply the prices charged by and prestige associated with attending one of the nation's "nifty-fifty" institutions—a term derived from the *U.S. News and World Report* rankings, the nation's most market dominant collegiate classification.

Not so coincidentally, our Stanford and Michigan colleagues at NCPI were making this connection a key element in the overall research strategy then being developed by the center. If the first imperative for a successful national center bid is a technical proposal that responds directly to the RFP, the second is a thematic approach to the research task. For NCPI that dominant theme became the increasing tensions between institutional perspectives on the one hand and entrepreneurial and enterprise strategies on the other. We summarized our approach in a schematic presenting the often-opposing faces of higher education—one drawing on the traditions of the academy, the other taking on the hues of U.S. enterprise.

We first presented this concept at the 1998 American Educational Research Association annual meeting, arguing that much of the tension troubling U.S. campuses derived from the conflict between traditional values and market perspectives. Faculty were increasingly voicing the grinding erosion of the personal autonomy that had made academic life a last redoubt for the inquisitive as well iconoclastic. Too often faculty were being told what and how to teach, and how to grade, as well as where to focus their research. Who was telling them? The answer was devastatingly simple: "It's the market that makes us do it!" Ironically, for all of their complaints, the nation's most successful faculty—at least in terms of their access to funds and the freedom to pursue their own interests—have proven to be the most successful at mastering markets: the competition for research funds, for job offers either for themselves or their students, and for administrative jobs in which the winners are those with the skills to better position themselves and market their institutions.

This argument also led to a set of research questions focusing on the need to better know the nature of the market for higher education in the United States. What drives the market? What is the nature and scope of consumer opinion? Which outcomes does the market reward?

Fruition

The present volume provides our answers to those questions. More particularly, it summarizes and documents our work for NCPI—the elaboration of the structure of the market for baccalaureate education and the linking of that structure to a set of measurable collegiate outcomes as expressed through the lives of an institution's recent graduates.

Chapter One begins with a restatement and recalibration of a nearly insatiable drive for revenues in general and for student-generated revenues in particular that has come to characterize U.S. higher education over the last quarter century. On the one hand the need for student-generated revenues reflects a substantial decrease in publicly appropriated funds for institutional operations. On the other hand the rising importance of student-generated funds in the economies of most institutions also shows that constantly rising prices have yielded complaints about—but little decrease in the demand for—a college education.

Chapter Two presents the fundamentals of our market taxonomy: what it tells us about the structure of the market, the model's technical attributes, and its capacity to explain pricing behavior. More important, it details the identification of the principal seams separating one market segment from another and how student aspirations help to organize the market—making clear that substantially more than price is involved.

Chapter Three uses the market taxonomy to explore other kinds of institutional differentiation and to ask the question: When do markets not matter? What emerges is an important portrait of higher education's key similarities and differences in terms of faculty-student ratios, the use of part-time faculty, the distribution of students by ethnicity, and the kind of expectations faculty have of their students.

The CRI is the focus of Chapter Four—what it measures and just as important, what it does not. We describe the range of values, practices, and abilities the CRI tracks, some of the technical results of the first two rounds of CRI administrations, and an estimate of the instrument's reliability and stability.

Chapter Five draws on our understanding of how markets link providers and consumers to explain the uses to which the CRI can be put by both institutions and prospective students. What does the CRI teach an institution about its signature in the marketplace? How different are those signatures? Do they differ within as well as across market segments? What ought student shoppers be looking for? Can one generalize the results from just eighty institutions to include most of higher education? The larger message is that higher education needs smarter shoppers, students-to-be who know more about the institutions they are considering than their place in the rankings, their reputations for throwing good parties, and the kinds of academic scores it takes to gain admission.

In a concluding chapter we return to our roots as institutional researchers and planners to translate our insights about the nature of the market into a set of axioms, rules, and practical tools that campuses can use in the search for answers to the questions they are increasingly asking: What is their market position? Is repositioning possible? Our hope is that this volume will provide a set of practical and theoretical constructs by which institutions can remain value centered by becoming market smart.

Robert Zemsky
Susan Shaman
Daniel B. Shapiro
Authors

ROBERT ZEMSKY is founding director of the Institute for Research on Higher Education, University of Pennsylvania, and professor and chair of Higher Education at the University of Pennsylvania.

SUSAN SHAMAN is the former assistant vice president for Planning Analysis at the University of Pennsylvania and currently serves as director of special projects for the Knight Higher Education Collaborative.

DANIEL SHAPIRO is the former director of research for the Institute for Research on Higher Education and currently is the chief information officer of the School of Dental Medicine of the University of Pennsylvania.

1

In the last twenty-five years colleges and universities have enjoyed unprecedented revenue growth. Using the revenue histories of seven institutions to highlight industry-wide trends, this chapter focuses on how the pursuit of revenue accelerated the shift from institutional to market perspectives across U.S. higher education.

Revenue

It is an observation delivered in earnest, usually by college or university presidents struggling to make their campuses more responsive to change: "It's the right message—we do have to become more efficient, more productive; but the language is all wrong. Constantly talking about the market sends the wrong signal—it's the wrong metaphor." By now our response is equally earnest. The market is not a metaphor—it is real, its discipline exacting, its impact on how colleges and universities function difficult to overestimate. How well an institution understands the workings of the market for postsecondary education—technically, rather than metaphorically—and its place in that market increasingly determines that institution's capacity to earn the revenue it needs to shape its own future.

The Making of the Market

Markets are hardly new to higher education. At the University of Pennsylvania, where most of our work has taken place, two of the most prized possessions in the university's archives are a pair of tickets—bought and redeemed—for medical lectures given at the end of the eighteenth century. It was how the university earned its keep. Such transactions represent a history that much of higher education in the United States has forgotten. Beginning in the last half of the twentieth century colleges and universities have been celebrated as institutions that are different; they are not given to buying and selling and only worry about prices and revenues when their public means of support diminish. Nonetheless, the processes by which colleges

This volume represents the views of the authors and not necessarily those of the Department of Education or the Knight Foundation.

and universities raise revenues are not different, not less commercial, not less subject to the basic constraints of supply and demand.

How can we be so certain that the phenomena we attribute to the commercial nature of the postsecondary market are not better explained by the competition among institutions for prestige and the bragging rights that go along with being named one of "America's Best Colleges"? Consider for a moment Japan's higher education system, which, although in many ways modeled after that of the United States, is even more ordered and competitive. In Japan a precise and widely understood pecking order exists among institutions; the top universities have the greatest share of funds to spend on their students and on themselves. Those top institutions are also in greatest demand, although almost no one in Japan talks about a market for higher education because demand does not translate into price. Indeed, the most prestigious, most sought after universities are the ones with the lowest prices.

That is not the case in the United States. Here, the equation reads: the greater the demand, the greater the number of applicants an institution can turn down, the higher the tuition that institution can charge. This rule holds even among public institutions. Market demand translates directly into increased revenue and hence an institution's capacity to be the master of its own fate.

Determinants of Revenue Growth

How did the market come to play such a central role in determining the revenues and therefore the shape of colleges and universities in the United States? The answer lies in a fundamental transformation that occurred in the financing of higher education that began shortly after World War II and then accelerated with the economic stresses and stagnation of the 1970s. To tell the story of this quiet revolution in the financing of colleges and universities, we drew on the financial data that these institutions annually submitted to the Higher Education General Information Survey (HEGIS) and now submit to its successor, the Integrated Postsecondary Education Data Systems (IPEDS). Both of these databases are located on the Computer-Aided Science Policy Analysis and Research (CASPAR) Web site hosted by the National Science Foundation (http://caspar.nsf.gov/). Using these data, we began defining four groups of baccalaureate institutions: (1) a set of highly selective, high-price private research universities, (2) their competitive peers among the nation's private liberal arts colleges, (3) a set of major public research universities, and (4) a set of public comprehensive institutions.

The two groups of private institutions included in the analysis compose the membership of the Consortium on Financing Higher Education (COFHE). The public research universities included represent all of the public members of the Association of American Universities (AAU). (All the private research universities included in the analysis also belonged to the AAU, although not all AAU private research universities were included.) The public comprehensive institutions represent all public doctoral and comprehensive colleges and universities that had consistently reported data first to HEGIS and subsequently to IPEDS.

The logic for selecting these particular sets of institutions was straightforward. Public research universities are often the flagships that set the pace for other campuses in their state systems, and the public comprehensives (along with community colleges) satisfy the bulk of the market for postsecondary education in the United States. The two groups of private institutions receive the preponderance of press coverage heralding each year's tuition increases. Indeed, these "Medallion" institutions frequently serve as the industry's price setters.

For each year during the period from 1975 to 1996 and for each institution in the four groups included in the analysis, we summed the *core revenues* they reported either to HEGIS or IPEDS. We defined *core revenues* as the following:

- Student tuition and fees (not including room, board, and other auxiliaries)
- Federal funds (principally, research grants and contracts but also federally supplied, institutionally based student aid funds)
- State and local grants, contracts, and appropriations
- Private gifts and grants
- Income earned by the institution's endowment

What happened to the core revenues of the four sets of institutions over this twenty-one-year period? In almost every case these colleges and universities enjoyed real revenue growth—that is, their core revenues increased faster than the underlying rate of inflation. Both private liberal arts colleges and research universities led the way, with annual average increases in core revenues of roughly 4 percent, in constant dollars (3.9 percent for highly selective private research universities; 4.2 percent for highly selective private liberal arts colleges; 2.7 percent for major public research universities; and 2.5 percent for public comprehensive universities).

Figure 1.1 shows the growth rates by institutional group at five-year intervals (1975 to 1995). For most of the 1980s the private and highly selective institutions enjoyed a substantial advantage. Not until the 1990s did the public institutions begin to catch up, although not fast enough to curtail the lead established by their highly selective private counterparts.

Note also that all growth rates are positive. Even in years when the public institutions lagged behind their private counterparts, on average they too enjoyed real increases in core revenues. What is also clear is that students and their families were responsible for higher education's good fortunes. Among the nation's most selective private institutions, tuition's share of core revenues grew at a steady pace: for the private, highly selective research universities

**Figure 1.1. Average Annualized Real Growth Rates
in Core Revenues in Five-Year Intervals**

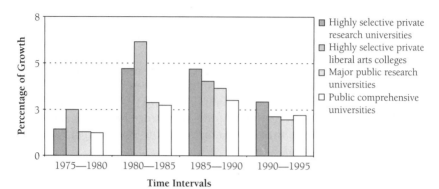

included in our analysis, the proportion of core revenues derived from student tuition and fees increased from an average of 27.2 percent in 1975 to 34.9 percent in 1996, and for the highly selective liberal arts colleges, the corresponding increase was from 52.3 percent in 1975 to 60.6 percent in 1996.

Although the initial percentage increases for public institutions were relatively smaller, the rate of growth in tuition's share of their core revenues was equally substantial. In 1975 major public research universities derived an average of 15.7 percent of their core revenues from tuition, and public comprehensive institutions drew an average of 19.8 percent. Twenty-one years later these averages were 24.6 percent and 33.4 percent, respectively, which translate into a nearly nine percentage point shift for the AAU public universities and a more than thirteen percentage point increase for the public comprehensives.

To further calibrate higher education's growing dependence on student-generated revenues, we turned next to a pair of comparisons between market-generated funds and those funds more traditionally associated with higher education: public appropriations and endowments. Examining the ratio of public appropriations to tuition revenue for public comprehensive and public research universities makes clear the magnitude of the shifts we are tracking. At the high watermark of public support during the close of the 1970s both types of public institutions were receiving approximately one dollar in tuition revenues for every three dollars in state and local appropriations. By 1996 that ratio would be halved. For every three dollars in state and local appropriations these public institutions were earning an additional two dollars from student tuition and fees.

A comparison of the share of core revenues from tuition versus endowment income provides an analogous measure for private institutions. From 1975 to 1979 highly selective liberal arts colleges received 1.8 tuition dollars for every dollar of endowment, while research universities received two tuition dollars for every one endowment dollar. Twenty-one years later selective liberal arts colleges were receiving more than three tuition dollars for every dollar of endowment; research universities were receiving nearly that amount, at 2.9 tuition dollars per endowment dollar.

Whereas higher education, particularly public higher education, had once been subsidized by the willingness of the many to support an opportunity enjoyed by only a few, a college education today is best understood as a private, even a consumer, good available to nearly everyone—although at radically different prices. As a result colleges and universities of every stripe are now largely on their own; even public institutions now rely on the market to fund their aspirations and operate their educational programs. Just as important, this shift in revenue sources has allowed the core revenues of all but a handful of institutions to outpace inflation each year. For a quarter century—year in and year out—most colleges and universities have enjoyed real and substantial revenue growth. Although dollars derived from research and service activities have also risen substantially over this period, the real story is that students and their families have shouldered an ever-larger share of the costs of operating the nation's colleges and universities. That's what made the market.

An Institutional Perspective

Presentations of aggregate data often obscure the eddies that roil individual institutions caught in the midst of the kind of transformation we are charting. On the other hand aggregate data are safer to use because aggregation smoothes the fluctuations introduced by errors in reported data at the institutional level. HEGIS and IPEDS, moreover, are notorious for this kind of error largely because the data the institutions report are seldom used for anything other than research. That caveat notwithstanding, we found it helpful to develop a series of minicases focusing on how these economic shifts played out in the histories of individual institutions.

In all we looked at seven institutions: three private highly selective research universities (Harvard University, University of Pennsylvania, Princeton University), two public AAU research universities (University of California-Berkeley, University of Michigan), and two public comprehensive institutions (Kent State University, San Francisco State University). The financial data summarized in Table 1.1 reflect the basic lessons we extracted from these institutions. They also indicate the following trends:

- All seven institutions enjoyed real revenue growth between 1975 and 1996; indeed, in all but a few cases each institution's revenues increased faster than the rate of inflation every year.
- Once more the rich got richer. Princeton, the richest university in the United States on a per-capita basis, led the parade, followed by Harvard

Table 1.1. Changes in Tuition and Fee Revenue, 1975–1996

Institution	Tuition and Fee as Percentage of Core Revenue, 1975	Tuition and Fee as Percentage of Core Revenue, 1996	Percentage Point Increase, 1975–1996
University of Pennsylvania	33.4	48.1	14.7
Kent State University	34.7	42.8	8.1
Harvard University	25.2	35.8	10.7
San Francisco State University	12.7	34.5	21.8
University of Michigan	19.7	34.0	14.3
Princeton University	28.8	32.8	4.0
University of California–Berkeley	14.3	23.4	9.1

and the University of Pennsylvania. All four public institutions enjoyed positive, but less robust, growth rates.

- Because they were more dependent on state tax revenues, the public institutions were more subject to fluctuations in the business cycle. The core revenues of the three private institutions seem to have not been affected by any of the downturns in the U.S. economy after 1981.

A slightly different, although still complementary, set of findings emerges when the lens focuses on actual dollar growth. The revenue figures demonstrate the ability of the University of Michigan and Harvard to put increased distance between themselves and their competitors. In real terms each institution nearly doubled its revenue over the twenty-one-year period. The University of Michigan, which stumbled at the beginning of the span and actually lost revenue between 1975 and 1982, recovered in the mid-1980s and then matched Harvard stride for stride in the race for increased revenues. The University of Michigan succeeded largely by making itself less dependent on funding from the state of Michigan and substantially more dependent on market-generated student tuition and fee revenue.

The details of the University of Michigan's revenue performance (see Figure 1.2) indicate the magnitude of the shift from state grants and contracts to tuition and fees. For this institution the percentage of core revenue derived from tuition and fee charges increased by 75 percent, from 19.7 percent in 1975 to 34.0 percent in 1996. The only other revenue category to increase its share was private gifts and contracts, and then only modestly. The share of core funding from the university's endowment remained con-

Figure 1.2. Changes in Relative Shares of
Core Revenue, University of Michigan

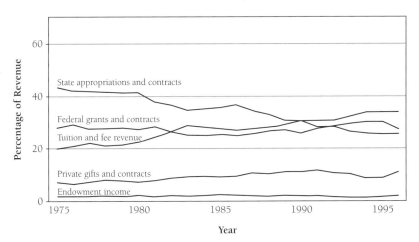

stant despite its increasingly successful capital campaigns. Federal funds also represent a constant share, no mean trick since Michigan's core funds were increasing overall by 2.5 percent in real dollars each year. The big drop occurred in funds supplied by the state of Michigan, a decline both in real dollars and in share of core revenues. By the late 1990s the state was actually supplying less than 20 percent of the university's total revenues (including the operation of its hospital and its auxiliary enterprises). The University of Michigan had become the face of privatization.

The experience of the University of California-Berkeley represents what happens when there is a sharp downturn in state support on the one hand and a sustained reluctance to increase student fees on the other (see Figure 1.3). For most of its history the University of California system had declined to charge students tuition, believing instead that as a public good, a college education ought to be provided by the state. In this respect the University of California resembled European and publicly funded Japanese universities. Faced with the need to increase revenues in order to remain competitive, the University of California first increased student fees; later, when confronted with a substantial reduction in funding from the state of California, it began to charge students a rapidly escalating tariff. If, however, the goal was to remain competitive with the University of Michigan and Harvard and ward off the escalating ambitions of institutions such as the University of Pennsylvania, then the price increases came almost a decade too late. By 1991, when the new policies were put into effect, the University of Michigan was already drawing 31 percent of its core revenues from student tuition and fee income. By the end of the decade the University of California-Berkeley was only drawing 23.4 percent from the same source even though its other sources of revenue largely mirrored those of the University of Michigan.

Figure 1.3. Changes in Relative Share of Core Revenue, University of California–Berkeley

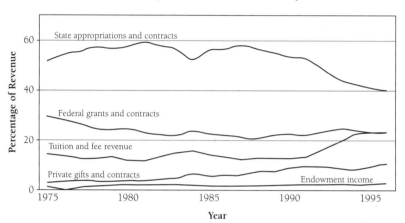

Princeton appears to be the exception to the trends (see Figure 1.4). Blessed with a highly focused set of undergraduate and graduate programs that include neither a school of medicine nor a school of law, Princeton enjoys an enviable market position, a substantial endowment, and a long history of raising both operating and capital funds from friends and alumni. It is also the one institution in our set that between 1975 and 1996 kept nearly the same relative balance among core sources of support. Princeton insulated itself from the turmoil of the market principally by making sure that endowment income matched student-market income. Figure 1.4 tracks an extraordinarily disciplined strategy that kept the university financially independent.

Because Kent State and San Francisco State lack both endowments and large programs of federally funded research, they illustrate more starkly the trade-off between state- and student-supplied funds. In both cases the shift to greater dependence on the student market as a source of operating funds was largely involuntary—the result of precipitous reductions in state funding that were in turn the result of downturns in the business cycle. In the case of San Francisco State, the 1990–1992 recession, which proved to be both more unexpected and more severe in California than elsewhere in the nation, ended a period of remarkable growth largely fueled by increasing state appropriations (see Figure 1.5). Since the recession San Francisco State, like the University of California-Berkeley, has been playing catch-up as it tries to restore its previous sense of momentum.

Hard times came earlier to Kent State, teaching it sooner the lessons of how to maximize student-supplied revenues. It was also one of the few comprehensive institutions able to translate its research aspirations into increased federal research support—a revenue source that by 1996 was supplying 10 percent of the university's core support (see Figure 1.6).

Figure 1.4. Changes in Relative Share of Core Revenues, Princeton University

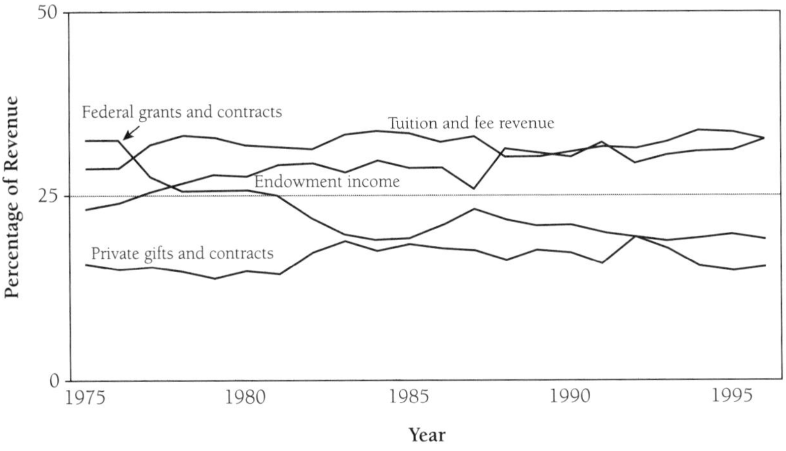

Federal grants and contracts

Tuition and fee revenue

Endowment income

Private gifts and contracts

Percentage of Revenue

Year

In each of these seven institutions, then, the basic story is the same. What allowed the three private universities to prosper and the public universities to recover, and at least in Michigan's case to recover and prosper, was their ability to increase student revenues.

Princeton provides an interesting footnote to this analysis. The only institution that did not receive at least a third of its core revenues from student tuition and fees in 1996, Princeton still saw its dependence on this revenue source increase by four percentage points over the two decades included in our analysis. Then in the spring of 2000 it announced its goal of a 10 percent increase in the size of its undergraduate student body to be accomplished over three years. Princeton was about to do what Harvard and the University of Pennsylvania had done a decade earlier: make the university more dependent on student-generated revenues as a means of funding its ambitions. In Princeton's case that ambition was tantamount to an 8 percent increase in the size of the university's standing faculty. Princeton had decided to go to the market.

Other Voices

We fundamentally believe that good numbers make for a good story, although in this case we understand that a good judge, when properly exercised, can do it better, or at least more succinctly. In 1991 the federal government charged that the Ivy Overlap group had restrained competition by agreeing to award the same financial aid to applicants admitted to two or more Ivy Overlap institutions. Of the more than 20 institutions charged, only the Massachusetts Institute of Technology (MIT) chose to fight the case, arguing in a trial before Judge Louis Bechtel that as a charitable institution MIT

Figure 1.5. Changes in Relative Share of Core Revenue, San Francisco State University

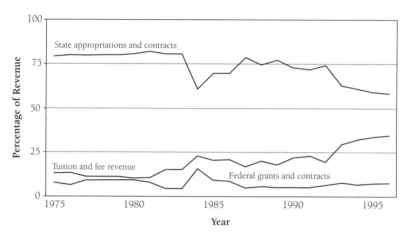

Note: Private gifts and grants and endowment income are negligible.

was not subject to the same antitrust laws as for-profit businesses. Indeed, MIT claimed that it was required to do all it could to keep its costs down, even if that meant entering into cooperative agreements with other institutions to set standard financial aid awards.

Labeling as "pure sophistry" MIT's contention that the distribution of financial aid was not a commercial endeavor, Bechtel noted: "MIT provides educational services to its students, for which they pay significant sums of money. The exchange of money for services is 'commerce' in the most common usage of the word (Goldfarb, 421 U.S. at 787–88, 95 S. Ct. at 2013). By agreeing upon the expected contribution of aid applicants' families, the Ivy Overlap Group was setting the price that students would pay for educational services. The court could conceive of few aspects of higher education that are more commercial than the price charged to students"(*United States v Brown University*, 805 F. Supp. 288 [E.D. Pa. 1992]).

Although his verdict was eventually reversed on technical grounds, Bechtel's characterization of higher education as an essentially commercial activity has always been true. Stanley Chodorow, medieval historian and former University of Pennsylvania provost, has argued that modern academics tend to forget that their universities have two roots. The first is the monastic school, a place of contemplation as well as labor, separate from worldly affairs. The second and in the end more dominant one was the medieval university, which grew as students flocked to Paris to attend the lectures of teaching masters. Addressing an All-University of California Conference on the Relationship Between Universities and Industry, Chodorow (1997) observed:

**Figure 1.6. Changes in Relative Share of Core
Revenues, Kent State University**

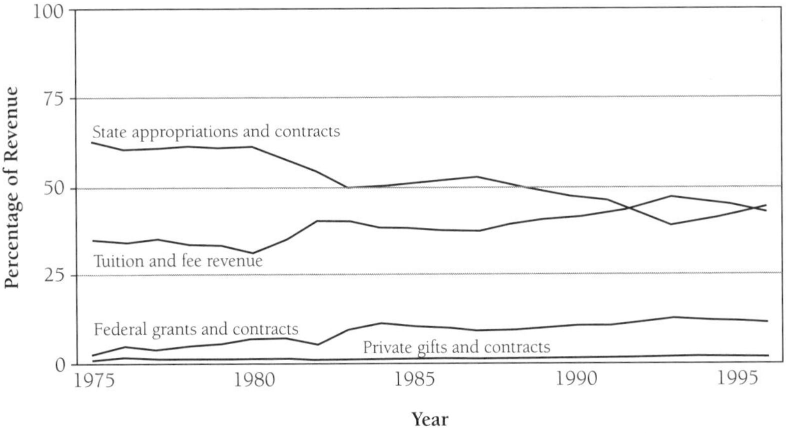

Note: Endowment income is negligible.

Where there were flocks of students, there was money to be made in teaching. Teaching masters soon came to Paris to take advantage of the opportunity that Peter Abelard and a few others had created. By the middle of the twelfth century, there were dozens of teachers and thousands of students, and, by the 1180s, it appears, the teaching masters there had formed the guild—the *universitas*—that would be the seed of the modern university.

The university was a craft guild, with the form and functions of all other craft guilds, [which] . . . organized and regulated the business of the teaching masters in the city. The guild was a collective entity, the very definition of a corporation. The teaching masters who belonged to the university made and sold knowledge. They made knowledge by applying logical analysis to the classic texts in grammar, philosophy, theology, medicine, and law. They sold this knowledge to students who came to take lectures and to get tutorial assistance.

For Bechtel and Chodorow institutions that maximize revenues, for whatever reason, are commercial enterprises. When the prices those institutions charge are themselves a function of demand, we are certain that what is at work is a competitive market for undergraduate students.

Not Just Here but Everywhere

In retrospect it is only remarkable that the growing dominance of market forces should have surprised anyone. What changed first and foremost for U.S. higher education after the headiness of the 1960s was that the pursuit of student-generated revenues came to play the dominant financial role in shaping the operations of most institutions. Colleges and universities, even the great public institutions on which the reputation of U.S. higher education often rests, were now expected to earn their own way.

A further irony is that some now think of these market trends as distinctly American. Yet, as with other vicissitudes that first emerge in the United States, what happened to higher education in the United States is rapidly becoming the new reality for other parts of the globe as well. A May 2000 story appearing in the *Chronicle of Higher Education* tells a strikingly familiar story: "The root cause of the pressure on the cost of college is the surge in demand for higher education worldwide. Over the past two decades, as national populations have risen, so has the proportion that completes secondary schools. That trend, coupled with a job market that keeps raising the bar in education, has created an enormous increase in the need for college-level training. But in most countries, public financing of higher education hasn't kept pace with that need, because of declining budgets and competing national goals" (Woodward, 2000, p. A54). What the rest of the world is discovering, and what U.S. institutions have known for nearly twenty-five years, is that when money matters, so do markets.

2

*This chapter introduces the authors' market
taxonomy, which reflects the structure of the
market for undergraduate education. The analytic
technique used to define the market segments is at
once intriguingly simple and demonstrably robust,
explaining why prices—and hence costs—vary
greatly across the market for baccalaureate
education in the United States.*

Segments

Markets and the choices confronting both buyers and sellers are at once
mysterious and straightforward—mysterious to those who believe markets
do not matter and reasonably straightforward once one accepts that the market is not a metaphor but a system of exchanges that shapes the enterprise.
It is in the nature and direction of those transactions that the structure of
the market is reflected.

The First Cut

In the early 1980s we developed our initial classification of the market for
undergraduate education in the United States for the College Board.
Focusing exclusively on the choices of high school seniors as they went
about the business of choosing a college, we developed a classification
scheme or taxonomy that placed most baccalaureate institutions in one of
four segments: national, regional, within-state, and local. As the names
given to each of the segments imply, we viewed our analysis as essentially
mapping the geographic mobility of applicants and the degree to which
individual institutions concentrated their recruiting efforts. Our definition
of a particular market, as in the Atlanta market, for example, drew on an
admissions officer's observation that he defined the boundary of any given
market as a circle whose radius was a two-hour drive in a rental car from
the region's airport.

Although that classification scheme used as its data the list of institutions to which individual high school seniors sent their SAT scores (regardless of whether they actually applied), one could not help but notice that the
resulting market segments also differed substantially by price. The national
segment proved to be the most expensive, and the local segment the least
expensive (Zemsky and Oedel, 1983). We returned to this observation with

a vengeance in 1997. By then we were asking the question: Could we segment the market for undergraduate education in the United States in terms
of price and demand, in line with our focus on markets and revenues? The
admissions officer's classic notion of selectivity as the product of admit rates
(how many applications an institution could turn down) and yield rates (how
many of its offers of admission were actually accepted) captured the basic
measure of demand we used. The data on admit and yield rates came from
the information most baccalaureate institutions report to one or more of the
major annual college guides: the College Board's *The College Handbook*,
Peterson's *Guide to Four-Year Colleges*, and Barron's *Profiles of American
Colleges*.

Once into the analysis, we discovered two problems. The first was that
a particular set of baccalaureate institutions offered educational products
that differed distinctly from all of the other institutions in our set. These
institutions appealed to student learners and customers who were acquir-
ing their baccalaureate degrees one course at a time, often from more than
one institution. We labeled these institutions as inhabiting the User-
Friendly/Convenience portion of the market. Analytically, we defined this
market cluster or segment as the set of institutions with more than one-
quarter of their students attending school part-time and with less than 15
percent receiving their baccalaureate degree in any given year (a term we
came later to define as an institution's *degree production ratio*).

The second problem was more intriguing and in the end proved more
essential to our understanding of the structure of the market for baccalaureate education in the United States. We were able to reasonably predict the
prices that individual institutions charge using our surrogate for demand.
Nonetheless, as many as 10 percent of the institutions were being placed in
the wrong segment because the admit and yield rates they reported had
clearly been inflated. They were what Susan Shaman came to call "our out-
liars," until one day she hit upon an ingenious solution to the problem. We
would introduce another term into our definition, one based on each institution's graduation rate—that is, the proportion of its freshman class that
was awarded baccalaureate degrees five years later. When added to the
demand measure, the screen produced the seven-segment market taxonomy
we published in *Change* in late 1997 (Zemsky, Shaman, and Iannozzi, 1997).

In that first presentation we described our market taxonomy as a horizontal, as opposed to a vertical, representation of the market, inviting our
readers to visualize a market structure that resembled a paper airplane (see
Figure 2.1). The airplane's right wing (segments 6 and 7) represents the User-
Friendly/Convenience part of the market served by institutions with substantial part-time enrollments. The left wing represents the Medallion/Name
Brand part of the market (segments 1, 2, and 3). The education offered
within this sector conforms to the traditional notion of a four- or five-year
undergraduate career frequently followed by the seeking of a graduate or professional degree. The airplane's fuselage represents the core of the market

Figure 2.1. Original Airplane Sketch Depicting Market Segments

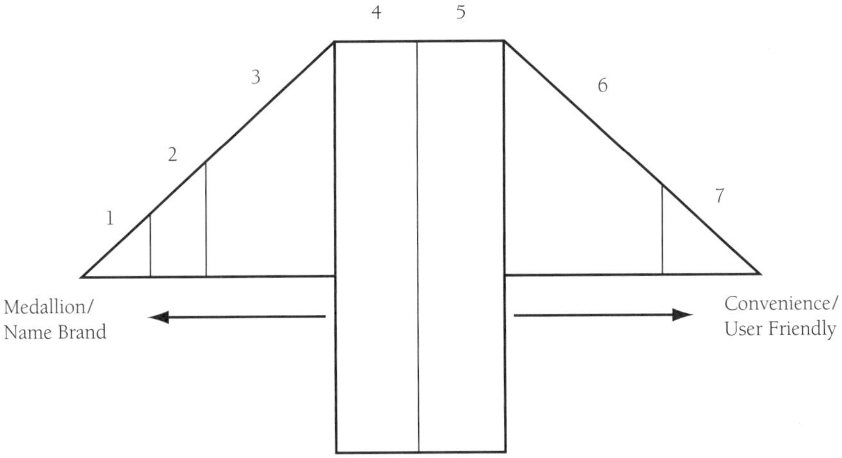

Source: Zemsky, Shaman, and Iannozzi, 1997.

(segments 4 and 5); some of these students sought Name Brand experiences while others pursued a baccalaureate education on a more intermittent basis.

Following the initial publication of this market taxonomy, a surprisingly large number of college and university presidents said that at least intuitively, the results made sense; their institutions had been placed in the correct market segment. Faculty were not quite so sure, particularly those whose institutions fell in less-lofty company than they thought they deserved. Higher education researchers, on the other hand, were substantially more prickly on the subject, asking for a justification for the individual cut points used to separate one market segment from another. We did not have a compelling answer, having picked them by a kind of jiggling process that chose and then tested different cut points to see if they made sense upon inspection.

We were also asked about the underlying meaning of our use of data reflecting the five-year graduation rate for each entering freshman. As part of the process to verify the model and analysis underlying the market taxonomy, we conducted regional meetings with members of the Knight Higher Education Collaborative. For the most part these meetings were attended by presidents, chief academic officers, and chief financial officers, often accompanied by an institutional researcher.

In addition to offering verification of our analytic process, the purpose of the meetings was to develop techniques for using in an institutional context the insights derived from the market taxonomy. The topic the discussions kept coming back to, however, was the extent to which the five-year graduation rate was proving to be a bellwether measure. As the taxonomy made clear, institutions seeking to reposition themselves in the market—moving, for example, from a core to a Name Brand segment—had to first improve their retention and, hence, graduation rates. Prospective students did not necessarily ask about the five-year graduation rate when shopping for colleges; rather, institutions with lower graduation rates had lower rates of retention and therefore had to admit more students to meet their enrollment goals. The more applicants an institution admitted, the less demand it enjoyed relative to the size of its freshman class. Put more simply, when an institution improved student retention, it would have to offer admission to fewer candidates, but it was more likely to prove attractive to those candidates it most wanted to enroll.

Redefining the Question

Those discussions led to a startling conclusion: in actuality, five-year graduation rates segmented the market. That realization in turn led to the search for a possible mechanism that somehow translated retention into demand, and demand into price. We began asking ourselves: For what underlying attribute is the five-year graduation rate a proxy?

First, did graduation rates predict price? The answer is a straightforward "Yes." That variable alone explains 44 percent of the price variance among the nearly one thousand institutions for which complete 1995 data was available. The percentage of an institution's freshmen who graduate in five years will indicate roughly the kind of tuition it charges and not so incidentally, how that institution is likely to score in the *U.S. News and World Report* rankings.

Why? The answer that slowly emerged was that the five-year graduation rate is really an aggregate measure of an institution's student body—the kinds of students it attracts, their commitment to completing their college educations, and their willingness to pay. When an institution year in and year out graduates more than 75 percent of its freshmen within five years, it is a signal that most students entered that institution almost certain they would graduate both on time and most likely from that institution. Institutions with five-year graduation rates closer to 50 percent were likely attracting more tentative learners, students for whom college might be a stretch, students who said, "I'll try it and see if I like it."

The image that helped us make sense of the numbers came from a high school physics lesson: all moving bodies have momentum, a forward glide they will maintain until something either blocks their way or provides an accelerating boost. High school students with a high propensity to enter and succeed in college—that is, high momentum—are attracted to those institutions with both higher barriers to admission and programs that often accelerate as well as focus the ambitions of their graduates. Students with less momentum most likely know they do not have enough speed to make it into the most selective and hence competitive institutions. They are also the students most likely to wonder if the nation's most competitive institutions are worth their high prices.

With this speculation as our working hypothesis, we turned to the task of rebuilding and then reverifying the market taxonomy we published in *Change*. That original market taxonomy tracked well with institutional "sticker price"—tuition and fees in the case of private institutions and the out-of-state tuition charged by public institutions. The problem was that most public institutions, although they have an out-of-state tuition on the books, actually attract very few out-of-state students. Then too, we had to consider financial aid. We had begun our market explorations worrying about the growing importance of discount rates in explaining what an institution actually charged. If no one or almost no one at an institution paid the sticker price, then it was not a true price at all. Finally, we had to consider the role that public appropriation plays in determining prices. In the original presentation of the taxonomy we noted that institutions within the same market segment, public as well as private, shared roughly the same level of expense per full-time equivalent (FTE) student. We concluded that it would probably be best to think about state appropriations as a kind of price support system in which public monies are used to offset the tuition revenue lost by the inability to charge a true market price.

The next step was to translate this logic into a dependent variable reflecting what we came to define as a "calculated price." For each of 958 institutions with complete data, we calculated a price equal to the sum of each institution's stated tuition (in-state for public institutions) plus any state appropriations per FTE student, minus all institutionally funded student financial aid per FTE. In the latter two cases—public appropriations and institutionally funded student financial aid—we had to make the assumption that the overall funds reported to IPEDS are allocated proportionally to undergraduate, graduate, and professional students based on FTE enrollments. Our analysis would have been neater if we had the actual amounts spent on undergraduates; that simply was not possible. The additional accuracy introduced into the analysis by using this calculated price, however, appears to us to outweigh the risk of substantial error.

Next, we turned to defining a set of independent variables—what we presumed would help in the prediction of price. To admit, yield, and five-year graduation rates we added the institution's location in one of six geographic regions (New England, Middle Atlantic, South, Midwest, Southwest, and West). In addition, we included the percentage of total undergraduate degrees granted in an institution's largest undergraduate degree program or major and the size of the undergraduate student body expressed as FTEs.

Why this set of variables? Our old friends admit rate and yield capture the link between price, selectivity, and market demand as reflected in the statement, "The more they want to come, the more they will likely pay." We included the percentage of an institution's graduates in its largest degree program or major in order to adjust for those institutions with a specialized focus. At engineering institutions, for example, students who become dissatisfied with their majors often have no other alternative but to transfer if they want to pursue other, particularly nonscientific, courses of study. The six regional variables take into consideration the effects of regional cost-of-living adjustments, whereas total FTEs help control for the size, and often the complexity, of an institution. Missing from this list is a public/private control variable. Although the original taxonomy used the same criteria and a single set of definitions to place institutions in market segments, we took the opportunity provided by the redefining of the taxonomy to specify separate models for each sector. The result was a set of parallel specifications that take better account of the differences between public and private institutions.

Soundings

To search for the boundaries separating the market into distinctive segments, we adopted a regression strategy that took its cue from sonar explorations of the sea bed. Oceanographers do not swim to the ocean floor to chart its depths; instead, they bounce sound waves back and forth, using the reflected returns to develop a picture of the bottom terrain. In similar fashion our analysis began with a series of reflected snapshots of today's market terrain for baccalaureate education. We used regression analysis as our sonar and our calculated price (sticker price plus appropriations divided by FTE, minus institutionally funded student aid divided by FTE) as the terrain marker.

We also began with the conjecture that where there are different market segments, the boundaries between two segments can be detected when the same regression model—that is, a model with the same dependent and set of independent variables—applied to two adjacent segments yields noticeably different parameter estimates. We tested this strategy against two data sets, one with 629 private institutions, the other with 329 public institutions.

The unexpected result is the negative sign associated with yield rates. The regression results displayed in Figure 2.2 tell us that all other things being equal, institutions with higher yields charge lower prices, a finding consistent throughout our analysis. Why? One explanation is that students and their families at the margins often chose the lower-priced alternative among a set of acceptable choices. If two institutions with nearly identical profiles charge different prices, the institution with the lower price will have the higher yield rate.

Another possible explanation lies in how institutions at a competitive disadvantage fill their classes: by harvesting each student one applicant at a time. For these institutions the trick is to focus their recruiting efforts on those students most likely to enroll. Therefore admit rate matters less because they admit nearly all of the applicants they have recruited—that is, all of the applicants with whom they have established a solid working relationship. Thus as admit rates rise, so do yield rates. As one of the presidents of this kind of institution explained the logic, "We know that if we can get them to apply we can get them to come."

We were now ready to plumb our distribution of private institutions, looking for the cut points that would establish the likely boundaries. First,

Figure 2.2. Predicting Calculated Price, Private Institutions

		Estimate*	Prob>|t|
RSquare	0.66		
Mean calculated price	$9,509		
Observations	629		
Intercept		8251.3	<.0001
Admit rate		−23.0	<.0001
Yield		−55.4	<.0001
Percentage in largest degree program		20.2	<.0001
Size		0.2	<.0001
Percentage receiving bachelor's degree in five years		62.5	<.0001
New England		1462.4	<.0001
Middle Atlantic		750.8	0.0001
South		−841.8	<.0001
Southwest		−878.5	0.0042
West		2007.7	<.0001

Note: Excluded category is Midwest.

*Shaded cells indicate significant at .05.

we sorted out the 46 institutions whose profiles identify them as competing principally in the User-Friendly/Convenience market segment—that is, institutions with at least 25 percent of their FTE student body attending part-time and with degree production ratios of 15 percent or less. We then ordered the remaining 583 private baccalaureate institutions in our data set highest to lowest according to their five-year graduation rates.

Next, we partitioned that ordered set into slices representing 5 percent intervals of five-year graduation rates: all institutions with graduation rates of 95 to 100 percent fell in the first slice; all institutions with five-year graduation rates at least 90 but less than 95 percent composed the second; and so on through the slice of institutions whose five-year graduation rates were at least 10 but less than 15 percent. (We omitted the handful of institutions whose reported graduation rates were below 10 percent.)

The next step was to combine these 5 percent slices into a set of moving bands (see Figure 2.3). We combined the first five slices into a single band containing all institutions whose five-year graduation rates were between 75 and 100 percent. That grouping became our first band. Next, we dropped off the leftmost slice containing the institutions with five-year graduation rates of 95 percent or more and added in the institutions with five-year graduation rates between 70 and 95 percent. This group of institutions became the second band in our analysis. We then continued across the continuum displayed in Figure 2.3, each time dropping the highest 5 percent slice of the previous band and adding the next-lowest 5 percent slice. We constructed fourteen bands using this procedure. We called this series of bands a "moving slider" and the subsequent analytic technique, Slider Analysis.

Figure 2.3. Slider Bands for Private Institutions Based on Five-Year Graduation Rates

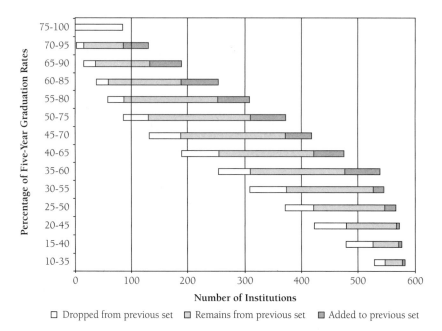

☐ Dropped from previous set   ☐ Remains from previous set   ■ Added to previous set

Using the same definition of price and the same set of predictor or independent variables specified in the model for private institutions (Figure 2.2), we reran the regressions using the data from each of the fourteen moving slider bands in turn and then plotted the resulting parameter estimates. We first applied the regression model to the band containing all private institutions whose graduation rates were at least 75 percent. We followed with the next regression, using data from institutions whose graduation rates were less than 95 but at least 70 percent. We continued in this way until we reached the last moving slider band, which included all institutions whose graduation rates were at least 10 percent but less than 35 percent.

Our objective was to examine the magnitude and statistical significance of the parameter estimates in each regression to observe how and for which bands the parameters changed. Figure 2.4 displays the plot of those regression estimates for the two variables that proved the most interesting: admit and yield rates. (The parameter estimate for size was also significant for most runs, but the estimate itself varied little over the bands.) The plot in Figure 2.4 is precisely what we were looking for—an indication of where the underlying model seems to indicate change or cut points.

For private institutions the three cut points, or boundaries, yielded four clusters on the chart. Moving left to right in Figure 2.4, the yield

Figure 2.4. Slider Analysis for Private Institutions

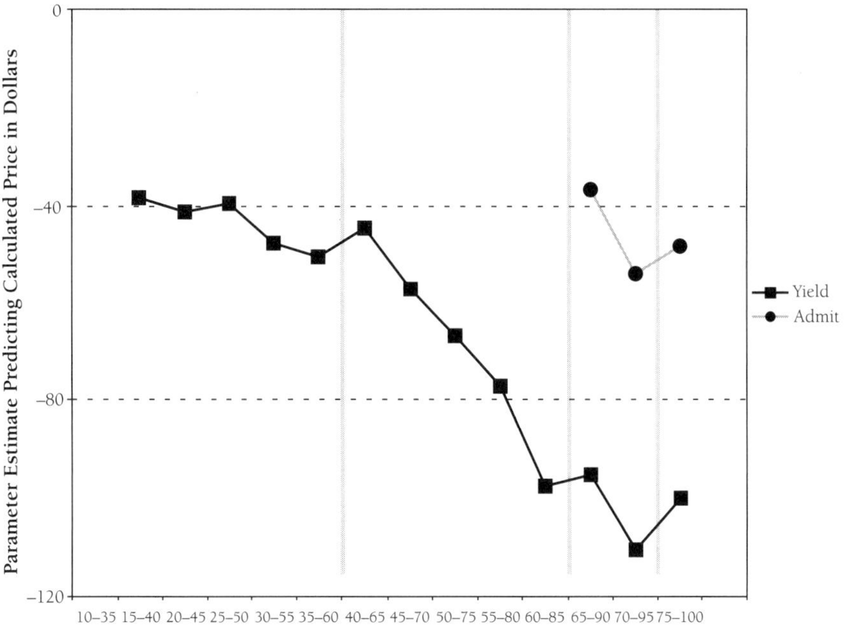

Percentage of Students Receiving Bachelor's Degree in Five Years by Slider Bands

Note: Does not include User Friendly/Convenience segment.

parameter estimates for the bands that included five-year graduation rates below 40 percent were both significant (at .05) and approximately the same size; that is, the line connecting the points is nearly flat. Yield is a significant predictor of price for this group with the estimate itself being relatively constant—about a $50.00 decrease in price for every percentage point increase in yield.

A change occurs when the slider band drops institutions with five-year graduation rates below 40 percent and starts including bands with rates over 65 percent. The parameter estimate linking yield and price becomes steadily more negative; that is, increases in yield lead to ever-sharper decreases in price. A further boundary appears when the slider crosses over and begins including in the analysis only institutions with graduation rates greater than 65 percent. Here, for the first time, admit rate becomes a significant parameter estimate.

The third and last boundary separates those institutions whose graduation rate is 75 percent or greater. Both the admit rate parameter estimate and the yield parameter estimate reverse direction. In this region changes in admit and yield rates lead to smaller changes in price, all other things being equal.

We make no claim for scientific precision. To a real extent the boundaries remain in the eye of the beholder—although as we will demonstrate, the four clusters or market segments based on these three boundaries differ in important ways. With these cautions in mind, we turn next to an analysis of the public institutions in our sample, again beginning by specifying a model that uses the same definition of price and set of predictor or independent variables we used in the Slider Analysis for private institutions (see Figure 2.5).

The differences are intriguing. In the public model none of the regional variables proved to be significant; in the private model all of the regional variables were significant. The power of the two analyses as expressed in terms of variance explained (or R^2) is less for the public model, suggesting that additional currents are at play in the public sector. Regardless, the basic shape is the same for both sectors. For both public and private institutions the calculated price increases as admit rate decreases; price also increases as yield rate decreases, probably for the same reasons described previously. In the public sector, as in the private, more highly specialized institutions charge higher prices. Again, in both sectors larger institutions are able to charge higher prices than smaller institutions. Finally, five-year graduation rates behave in roughly the same way in both sectors. Price increases as the five-year graduation rate increases.

When we turn to the Slider Analysis, the picture for the public institutions is decidedly less clear (see Figure 2.6). In the public, as opposed to the private, plot we have included all of the points that are significant at the 0.1 level and added a dotted line connecting the parameter estimates for yield, even for those estimates that did not prove to be significant at the 0.1 level.

Again, the plot allows nothing more than a visual interpretation. To our eyes something first happens when the boundary at five-year graduation rates exceeds 35 percent; at that point five-year graduation rate, size, and the percentage of an institution's students in its largest degree program are all significant at the 0.1 level. The final boundary is crossed when the five-year graduation rate exceeds 60 percent. At that point both size (FTEs) and specialization (percentage of students in the largest degree program) lose their significance, leaving only yield among this set of variables as a significant predictor of an institution's calculated price.

For us, the most interesting variable proved to be yield, which behaves fundamentally differently at the left as opposed to the right of the chart in Figure 2.6. This shift is not surprising, however; the most prestigious major public universities have come to practice selective admissions by discouraging—as opposed to encouraging—applicants who do not meet their announced qualifications (numeric criteria such as class rank, grade point average, and SAT or ACT scores).

Interestingly, a number of Big Ten universities had complained that our original analysis had given too much weight to admit rates. Given the number of students these institutions admit each fall, they have little interest in

Figure 2.5. Predicting Calculated Price, Public Institutions

		Estimate*	Prob>|t|
RSquare	0.38		
Mean Calculated Price	$8,230		
Observations	329		
Intercept		8902.3	<.0001
Admit rate		−39.8	<.0001
Yield		−20.7	<.0001
Percentage in largest degree program		51.7	<.0001
Size		0.1	<.0001
Percentage receiving bachelor's degree in five years		17.5	0.0478
New England		−133.0	0.7871
Middle Atlantic		170.6	0.6988
South		−58.8	0.8580
Southwest		−770.1	0.0803
West		−594.2	0.1158

Note: Excluded category is Midwest.

*Shaded cells indicate significant at .05.

decreasing their admit rates by having candidates apply whom they know will later be denied admissions. Basically, the Slider Analysis is telling us that these presidents were right; for their institutions the best measure of their market demand is their yield rate. At the tail of the distribution, where graduation rates are less than 45 percent, yield is most likely significant for the same reasons yield proved significant for the nonselective part of the private sector.

Defining Market Segments

The seven clusters identified through the Slider Analysis plus those containing the User-Friendly/Convenience part of the market become the basis for defining five pairs of market segments. We start with the private sector in which the five market segments are defined in the following way:

1. *User-Friendly/Convenience*. Part-time students make up at least 25 percent of the undergraduate student body and the institutions' undergraduate degree production ratio is less than 15 percent. In this segment graduation rates tend to be low, but we ignore the five-year graduation rate.
2. *Good Opportunity*. Institutions with five-year graduation rates less than 40 percent.
3. *Good Buy*. Institutions with five-year graduation rates greater than or equal to 40 percent but less than 65 percent.
4. *Name Brand*. Institutions with five-year graduation rates greater than or equal to 65 percent but less than 75 percent.

Figure 2.6. Slider Analysis for Public Institutions

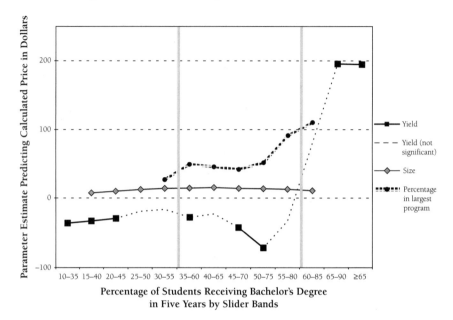

Note: Does not include User Friendly/Convenience segment.

5. *Medallion.* Institutions with five-year graduation rates greater than or equal to 75 percent.

The public-sector market segments parallel those of the private sector as follows:

1. *User-Friendly/Convenience.* Identical to the private sector criteria, part-time students make up at least 25 percent of the undergraduate student body and the institution's undergraduate degree production ratio is less than 15 percent.
2. *Good Opportunity.* Institutions with five-year graduation rates less than 35 percent.
3. *Good Buy.* Institutions with five-year graduation rates greater than or equal to 35 percent but less than 60 percent.
4. *Medallion/Name Brand.* Institutions with five-year graduation rates grea

ter than or equal to 60 percent for Name Brand institutions, combined with graduation rates above 75 percent for Medallion institutions.

The number of public institutions falling into the Medallion category was insufficient to define a separate segment for them, although 20 public universities among the 329 public institutions included in the analysis had graduation rates greater than or equal to 75 percent.

Once again, it is important to note that we have described market segments not rankings. The student customers who shop in one segment differ substantially from those who shop in another; hence the institutions they consider differ as well. To further dispel the notion that our market taxonomy is simply a dressed-up ranking system, we have named each segment by its dominant competitive characteristic, each time selecting a title that conveys what is attractive to students who shop in that particular segment.

- *User-Friendly/Convenience.* This is the one segment in which part-time as well as intermittent learners seem to dominate. Students in this segment often shop for a friendly environment at an institution that understands their special needs, including the need to take courses at times that are truly convenient.
- *Good Opportunity.* This segment is composed of institutions and students who often see higher education as a special opportunity. Many of the students who shop in this segment are the first in their families to attend college.
- *Good Buy.* This segment includes a variety of institutions that for the most part offer full-scale undergraduate programs at prices often substantially less than those at institutions practicing selective admissions.
- *Name Brand.* This segment is populated by well-known institutions— hence the moniker "Name Brand." Most of these institutions practice selective admissions, although their appeal is more likely to be regional than national. Many, but by no means all, of these institutions would like to be considered Medallion institutions.
- *Medallion.* The nation's most competitive institutions and most competitive students constitute this segment, a segment for which prestige-based rankings such as those annually published by *U.S. News and World Report* have played an ever-increasing role in defining institutional ambitions and hence quality.

The Market's Terrain

The differences between the market segments reflect the structure of the market. Again, we used a pair of regression analyses (one for private and one for public institutions) using the same set of predictor or independent variables to predict the prices institutions charged in each segment. Figure 2.7 presents this information for the five private market segments. As one would expect, the mean calculated price for each segment decreases when moving left to right (beginning with Medallion), with the exception of the User-Friendly/Convenience segment, which is actually on average more expensive than the Good Opportunity segment. We suspect that this exception is slightly misleading because students in the User-Friendly/Convenience

Figure 2.7. Predicting Calculated Price by Market Segment, Private Institutions

	Medallion*	Name Brand*	Good Buy*	Good Opportunity*	User Friendly/ Convenience*
RSquare	0.61	0.54	0.52	0.46	0.64
Mean calculated price	$12,590	$10,586	$8,728	$7,269	$7,974
Observations	109	112	291	71	46
Intercept	7800.5	11,585.5	60,18.7	4804.5	5619.4
Admit rate	−52.5	−4.4	−5.8	−23.6	19.6
Yield	−111.9	−95.5	−47.4	1.1	−23.5
Percentage in largest degree program	8.7	17.3	28.9	9.6	27.4
Size	0.2	0.3	0.4	0.0	0.4
Percentage receiving bachelor's degree in five years	126.5	13.0	64.1	87.2	31.4
New England	796.9	1020.1	18,58.1	3414.6	1440.9
Middle Atlantic	855.4	655.4	397.0	1518.6	832.9
South	−625.9	−936.9	−845.1	−517.0	−2175.1
Southwest	−3732.1	−1457.6	−771.5	−365.1	−1399.6
West	514.0	1886.5	1913.8	2186.6	

Note: Excluded category is Midwest.

*Shaded cells indicate significant at .05.

segment are more likely to purchase their educations "by the glass" (attending part-time) than "by the bottle" (attending full-time), thus spending less per semester than the typical student in the Good Opportunity segment.

What do we know about the structure of the private sector and its competition for undergraduate students? Admit rate, the quintessential measure of market demand in the private sector, becomes a significant predictor of price only in the left-hand side of the market as shown in Figure 2.7. On the right-hand side that role is played by the five-year graduation rate, which we believe fundamentally reflects the momentum student shoppers possess as they contemplate their college choices. Size is also an important predictor for the right-hand side of the market. The regional variables—included to control for regional cost variations—represent a mixed bag for which a coherent interpretation is difficult.

The terrain map for the public sector is remarkably similar (see Figure 2.8). Again, the mean calculated price decreases from left to right except for the slightly higher prices in the *User-Friendly/Convenience* segment, a market niche that again incorporates a truly separate market segment. The segment models for the public sector are less powerful (they have lower R^2 values) than for the private sector. The models also indicate that the Good Opportunity segment least fits the general model, although the reasons for this are not clear.

Not surprisingly, the combined public Medallion/Name Brand segment closely resembles its private counterpart. Admit rate and yield play the expected roles; none of the regional variables proved to be significant, and the general model worked best for this segment. In other words, the variance explained (R^2 value) is nearly identical for the public Medallion/Name Brand combined segment as it is if we combine the private Medallion and Name Brand segments.

The real pay-off lies in the corresponding values of the mean calculated price—that is, the sticker price plus state/local appropriation per FTE minus institutionally funded student aid per FTE for each segment. Only the combined private Medallion/Name Brand segment has substantially more revenue per student, about $1,130 more, than public institutions competing in the same market segment—a difference that could yet prove politically important.

The graph in Figure 2.9 shows just how well these values track one with the other as well as their consistency across market segments: public and private institutions competing against each other in most market segments will have roughly the same amount of student-provided plus government-appropriated funds to spend on their undergraduates.

A Whole Greater Than Its Parts

Our analysis of the structure of the market is now complete—we have specified the boundaries separating the segments, determined the procedures used, and defined the principal characteristics of each segment. When added

Figure 2.8. Predicting Calculated Price by Market Segment, Public Institutions

	Medallion* Name Brand*	Good Buy*	Good Opportunity*	User Friendly/ Convenience*
RSquare	0.57	0.32	0.27	0.43
Mean calculated price	$10,232	$8,296	$7,091	$7,739
Observations	49	153	71	56
Intercept	14,698.2	8157.2	11968.8	6018.8
Admit rate	-101.4	-10.5	-27.4	-34.9
Yield	34.6	-28.8	-37.5	1.6
Percentage in largest degree program	102.8	34.8	-11.2	68.5
Size	0.1	0.1	0.0	0.3
Percentage receiving bachelor's degree in five years	-58.7	-8.7	40.6	22.2
New England	848.8	421.5	-4661.3	727.6
Middle Atlantic	-643.1	1384.7	-1696.3	-396.2
South	177.0	310.5	-2095.4	439.3
Southwest	775.1	-884.8	-1792.3	817.0
West	734.6	-474.2	-1700.0	-1791.6

Note: Excluded category is Midwest.

*Shaded cells indicate significant at .05.

Figure 2.9. Mean Calculated Price by Market Segment and Control

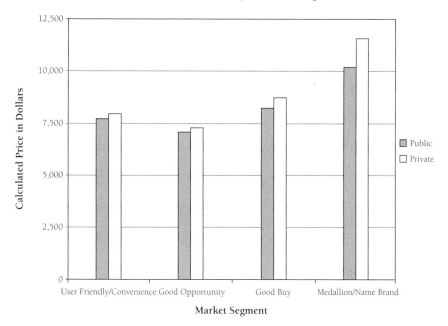

to our previous work, we can easily catalogue what we have learned. While there are basic similarities, important differences appear between the structure of the market for public and private institutions. The public structure looks most like that of the private structure on the left-hand side of the market—among the public Medallion/Name Brand institutions that, among other things, have been the most aggressive in raising their prices and thus taking advantage of their market positions.

3

In setting prices, markets determine the revenue available to institutions and as a result, shape institutional characteristics. This chapter tours the various market segments, demonstrating how faculty salaries, faculty-student ratios, use of part-time faculty, and—not coincidentally—student choice follow the ordering of the market. Teaching practices, on the other hand, appear to be invariant across market segments.

Contours

The danger inherent in any classification scheme is that it can be reduced—as in fact, college rankings have already been reduced—to a glorified parlor game. Everyone wants to peek to see who is and who is not a Medallion, to identify which institutions are on the rise, and to determine which are likely to have futures that match neither the grandeur nor the expectations of their pasts. For an industry that often shuns the language of the market because of its focus on winners and losers, the academy has had a long history of keeping score. How many Nobel laureates or National Merit Scholars can you boast of? How many Guggenheims or Pulitzers or National Championships have you won? It is this mania on which those who publish the rankings feed.

Although our interest in the market taxonomy was not necessarily more noble, it was at least different. Our goal was to calibrate how and when the structure of the market impacts learning outcomes. As part of that goal we have used the taxonomy to demonstrate how from the mid-1970s onward markets, and not costs, have determined the prices U.S. colleges and universities charged.

What the Market Explains

We begin with prices and their trajectories over the last twenty-five years. Of particular interest is the growing spread among the average sticker prices across each market segment (see Figure 3.1). In 1970 the most expensive institutions were charging on average 5.5 times as much as the least expensive ones. By 1990 that gap had increased to a multiple of 7.9 before receding to 6.8 in 1995, as public institutions began their own accelerated price increases. Leading the parade throughout the period were the private Medallion universities and colleges, followed by private Name Brand institutions. After 1990

Figure 3.1. Tuition by Market Segment and Control

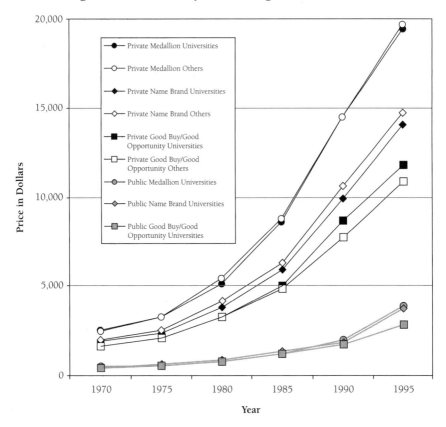

all three groups of private institutions—Medallion, Name Brand, and Good Buy/Good Opportunity—became more prudent in their price increases but not so prudent as to limit their hikes to match the rate of inflation.

What they lacked in rates of increase public institutions often made up through increased volume (see Figure 3.2). Between 1970 and 1995 the median undergraduate enrollment at public Medallion universities increased by 80 percent, and the median undergraduate enrollment at public Name Brand universities increased by 40 percent. Even among public Good Buy and Good Opportunity institutions, the median size of the undergraduate student body in these segments increased by 34 percent.

Once again, however, it was the rich who got richer. At private Medallion universities the average undergraduate enrollments increased by more than 28 percent, gains above and beyond price increases that were exceeding inflation by an average of three to five percentage points per year. At all other private Medallion institutions, for the most part highly selective liberal arts colleges, the median enrollment increased by 15 percent, and these institutions also benefited through robust price increases. Still, not

Figure 3.2. Enrollment by Market Segment and Control

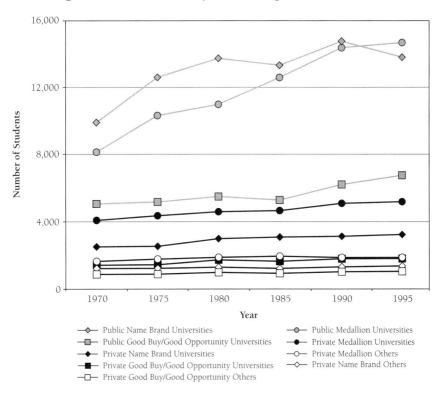

everyone could take advantage of a market environment that had magnified the underlying demand for a college education. While managing to show a small median enrollment increase, private Name Brand colleges found themselves settling for a constantly decreasing share of the market.

The median undergraduate enrollments shown in Figure 3.2 do not reflect the most surprising, as well as revealing, findings. Although the median undergraduate enrollment at private Good Buy/Good Opportunity institutions increased modestly over the twenty-five-year period, the variance among institutions was substantial. Whereas some institutions lost enrollment over the period, others, having mastered the tools of marketing and coming to understand the role creative pricing could play, increased the size of their student bodies an average of up to 7 percent per year—no mean feat for these small, often undersized campuses. Most public institutions in these same market segments also experienced enrollment growth, but they also lost ground and market share to better-positioned public and private competitors. The most ready explanation for this latter phenomenon is that during boom times students and their families "shopped up," opting for more selective, as well as more expensive, alternatives.

Alongside price and size, the structure of the market also helps explain the composition of baccalaureate institutions, particularly in terms of the race and ethnicity of their undergraduate students (see Figure 3.3). We suspect that no one will be surprised to learn that larger proportions of African American and Hispanic students than white and Asian are found in the Good Opportunity and User-Friendly/Convenience segments. Most troubling, however, is how strongly these distributions seem to be etched into the postsecondary landscape, suggesting that despite a quarter century of focus on improving access to higher education, one's color remains a key predictor of place of enrollment. The one group that has clearly broken the pattern is Asian Americans, whose distribution now mirrors that of most ethnic groups that have made a college degree a primary lever to social mobility. By 1995 45 percent of all Asian American undergraduates were enrolled in either a Medallion or Name Brand institution (private or public). The corresponding figures were 30 percent for whites, 19 percent for Hispanics, and 14 percent for African Americans.

Figure 3.3 also makes clear the extent to which the Good Buy segments constitute the core of the market. For all four ethnic groups Good Buy is the part of the market to which most Americans go. Almost by definition Good Buy institutions have reasonable prices, display a comfortable local or regional feel, and enjoy academic reputations that more than satisfy the ambitions that have led to the massification of U.S. higher education.

The distribution of three additional attributes is equally important to higher education: faculty salaries, student-faculty ratios, and the use of part-time faculty. To highlight the differences reflected in these distributions, we have divided the institutions in our analysis into three basic groups: all public institutions, all private liberal arts colleges, and all other private institutions. We then further subdivided each by market segment: five segments for the public institutions (Medallion, Name Brand, Good Buy, Good Opportunity, and User-Friendly/Convenience) and five segments for each of the two groups of private institutions (Medallion, Name Brand, Good Buy, Good Opportunity, and User-Friendly/Convenience).

The most intuitive finding is the ordered relationship between market segment and average faculty salary (see Figure 3.4). Institutions competing in market segments with the highest average prices and the most robust applicant pools pay their faculty the best average salaries. (In Figures 3.4 through 3.6 the heavy black lines plot the median for the distribution—in this case, average salaries. The vertical bars represent the spread between the 75th and 25th percentiles.) For the All Other Private: Medallion category, which is principally composed of the nation's best-known private research universities, the median average salary in 1996 for tenure-track faculty of all ranks was just under $75,000 per year. At the upper 25 percent of these universities the average salary was more than $83,000, and in the lower 25 percent faculty salaries averaged $70,000 or less.

Although equally ordered, the range of median average faculty salaries for the public market segments is considerably more compressed than it is for

Figure 3.3. Distribution of Undergraduates
by Segment and Race/Ethnicity (1995)

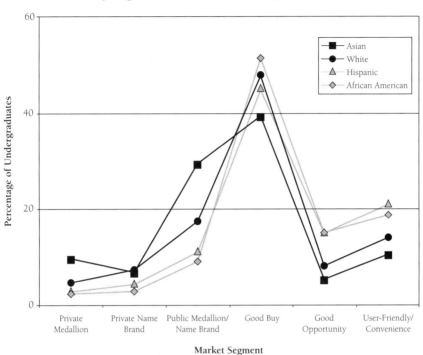

either of the two sets of private institutions. Perhaps this trend reflects that salaries at public colleges and universities in most states are a matter of public record and that these institutions are much more likely to have collective bargaining agreements. Faculty in public institutions are likely to be paid as well as if not better than their colleagues teaching in comparable institutions in the same market segment. The lowest in salary distribution proved to be faculty at liberal arts colleges. In the three less-selective market segments median faculty salaries on liberal arts campuses were actually below salaries at the 25th percentile for public institutions and well below the median for other private institutions competing in the same market segment. Even faculty at Name Brand and Medallion liberal arts colleges placed a full notch below their colleagues at other private institutions in the same market segment and half a notch below faculty at similarly positioned public institutions.

In part these lower salaries reflect the enrollment and hence price pressures facing liberal arts colleges, and in part they represent a deliberate trade-off between numbers of faculty and compensation. Liberal arts colleges advertise greater student-faculty interaction, achieved through lower student-faculty ratios; in the case of Medallion liberal arts colleges, student-faculty ratios are on average nearly five students per faculty member lower than any other institution (see Figure 3.5). Lower student-faculty ratios may

**Figure 3.4. Median Salary for Tenure-Track Ranks:
Assistant Professors and Higher (1997)**

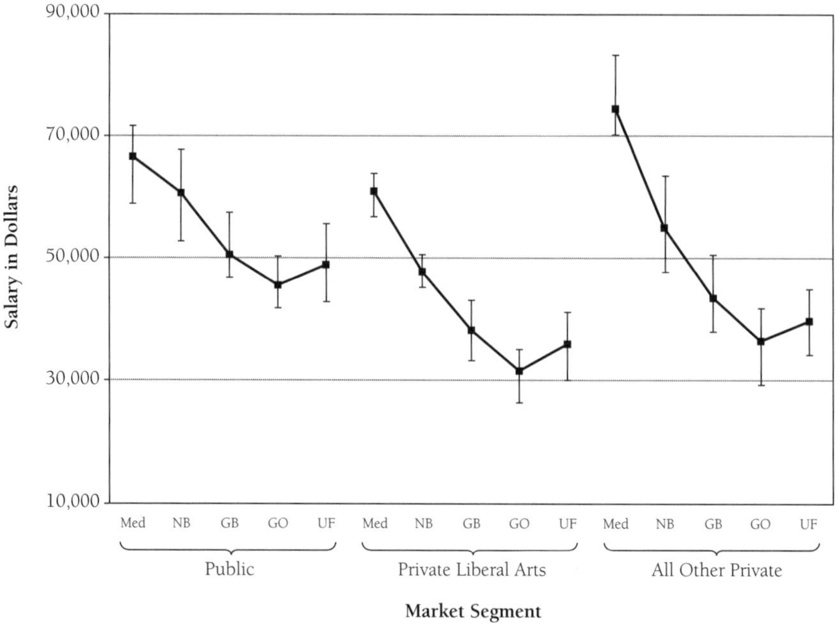

Note: Med = Medallion; NB = Name Brand; GB = Good Buy; GO = Good Opportunity; UF = User-Friendly/Convenience.

also be a function of underenrollment, as well as the need for these colleges to cover more disciplines in their academic programs as they face increased competition from institutions offering broader curricula and greater options.

Public institutions occupy the opposite end of the spectrum, having made competitive salaries a first priority. Here, too, the underlying dynamic is no doubt economic. Focusing on the calculated price (tuition minus institutional financial aid, plus endowment income, plus state appropriation), public institutions on average receive between $200 and $450 per student less than their private competitors in the same market segment. For a comprehensive institution with five thousand undergraduates competing in the Good Buy segment, the difference between the public and private calculated price is more than $400 per student, which translates into more than $2 million in revenue, enough to hire an additional thirty faculty.

The use of part-time faculty follows the expected pattern: fewer in the Medallion and Name Brand segments and most in the Good Opportunity and User-Friendly/Convenience segment (see Figure 3.6). Most remarkable, in some institutions the part-time faculty cadre is as large or larger than the full-time faculty. Moreover, within the All Other Private Good Opportunity segment, half the institutions reported hiring one part-time faculty for every two full-time faculty, and in the User-Friendly/Convenience category, one

Figure 3.5. Median Student-Faculty Ratio (1997)

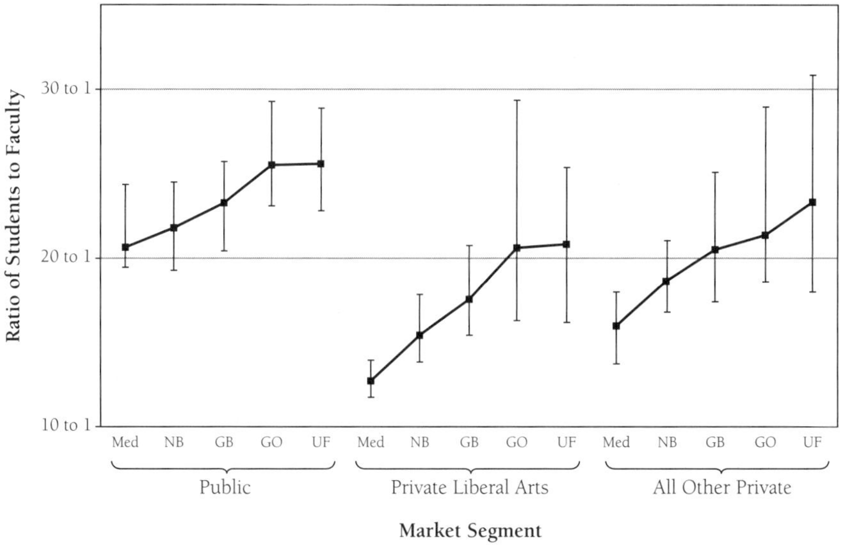

Note: Med = Medallion; NB = Name Brand; GB = Good Buy; GO = Good Opportunity; UF = User-Friendly/Convenience.

out of four institutions reported similar ratios. Again, economics and the need to diversify offerings as well as time and place of instruction explain this part of the market's use of part-time faculty at such a high rate. Part-timers cost less, fill niches, and understand the necessity of teaching when and where students in this market segment want to take their courses.

What the Market Does Not Explain

When the focus is on markets and prices, the substance of what faculty and students do, either separately or together, in pursuit of learning outcomes too often gets lost. Indeed, an important part of the story we are trying to tell is when and where faculty in institutions belonging to different segments teach differently and just as important, when they teach the same. Our analysis allows a sharpening of expectations before turning to the direct analysis of collegiate results.

Do faculty in different kinds of institutions really teach that differently? Do they make different kinds of assignments, assess their students in a different manner? Do they expect more or less of their students? Do they spend more or less time preparing for and administering their courses?

We started with the presumption that differences in market segments and hence prices and revenues ought to reflect differences in the educational product. It is this claim that institutions with superior market positions often make when defending the higher prices they charge: that what the student

Figure 3.6. Percentage of Part-Time Faculty (1997)

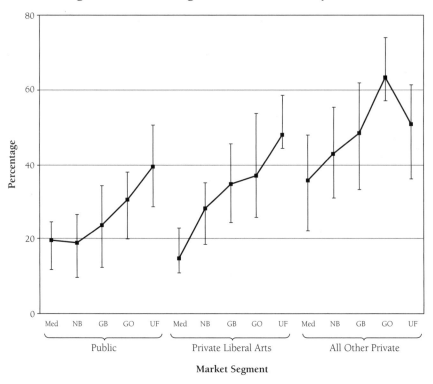

Note: Med = Medallion; NB = Name Brand; GB = Good Buy; GO = Good Opportunity; UF = User-Friendly/Convenience.

pays for is both a better and a different educational experience. Those differences ought to include what faculty do before a course begins, how they prepare for the daily challenge of the classroom, how they administer their courses and assess the progress of their students, and how frequently they interact with students outside of the classroom.

To explore this line of inquiry, we asked ten institutions to let us interview their faculty about instructional practices. For each institution we identified a set of courses from a sample stratified by discipline and then asked the faculty member who taught that course in the target semester to participate in a thirty-minute telephone interview. The interview began with the faculty member reporting how often he or she had taught this course previously and roughly describing its methodology—for example, if the course was team taught.

For the most important part of the interview, we asked each faculty member to characterize his or her activity for the course in terms of a series of tasks undertaken during three distinct time periods: prior to the academic term, during the term, and subsequent to the term. The time-period rubric served as a useful way to help faculty recollect their efforts. However, to create composite variables that were useful in an analytic framework, we grouped the responses into five general categories: (1) advance planning and preparation (planning), (2) student interactions (transactions), (3) preparation time for class (delivery), (4) assessing student performance, and (5) course administration.

We also asked faculty members to estimate the importance of three sets of academic goals for their particular course: the teaching of communication skills, the teaching of general learning and conceptual skills, and the teaching of computer and technical skills. Faculty responded to three related questions about each of these course goals: the amount of in-class time students spent pursuing the particular goal, the amount of out-of-class time students spent pursuing the particular goal, and the level of importance mastering that goal was to student success in the course. In framing their answers faculty members could choose a value on a scale of one to five, with one indicating "no time" or "not relevant" and five indicating "a great deal of time" or "very important." We then averaged responses to the questions on course goals to form three composite index variables.

We make no claims regarding the statistical representativeness of our sample of colleges and universities. We recruited the participating institutions because we knew their administrations to have an interest in determining the underlying cost of the undergraduate education they offered. Nonetheless, the spread of institutions is broadly representative of the market segments that are the focus of this study: three private Medallion research universities, one public Medallion research university, two private liberal arts colleges from a combined Medallion/Name Brand segment, and four institutions (a mix of private and public) from a combined Good Buy/Good Opportunity segment of the market. The sample included no User-Friendly/Convenience institutions.

The faculty surveyed from each institution did, however, constitute a statistically representative sample. At the liberal arts colleges we interviewed all faculty who taught courses in a target term about their specific course section. At the other institutions we limited the interviews to faculty who taught an undergraduate course in one of the following nine academic domains: business, chemistry, economics, engineering, English, fine arts, history, mathematics, and Romance languages.

In all, 401 faculty members completed interviews: 127 at private Medallion research universities; 45 at the public Medallion research university; 117 at Medallion/Name Brand liberal arts colleges; and 112 at the combined Good Buy/Good Opportunity institutions. We consider the institutional response rates in our voluntary survey—ranging from a low of 31 percent to a high of 67 percent and averaging 48 percent overall—to be quite acceptable.

As we had hoped, the survey instrument proved to be a rich source of detailed information on how faculty organize their teaching, what they expect of their students, how they spend their teaching time, and what kinds of goals they set for themselves and for their students. We better understand when and how teaching varies across disciplines and by rank, as well as the role that the structure of the curriculum plays in shaping the context in which learning takes place.

Our focus here, however, is the question with which we began this section: To what extent can the market explain differences in teaching practices that cannot be accounted for in terms of discipline and level of instruction? Do faculty at institutions that serve one part of the market as opposed to another expect more or less of their students? Do they invest their teaching time differently? Do they emphasize different concepts or skills in their teaching goals?

We begin with an index reflecting the amount of time faculty at each of the ten institutions devoted to one of our five basic teaching activities, in order of activity: planning the course, preparing in-class instruction (delivery time), assessing student performance, administering the course, and spending time with students outside of class (transaction time). Overall, the graph in Figure 3.7 reflects a jumble of results, perhaps the product of the small sample but more likely demonstrating that market order does not govern these aspects of an undergraduate education. In all four segment groupings course administration is a minimal constant. In general, the faculty in the combined Good Buy/Good Opportunity segments reported spending the least time per course on three of the five tasks, most likely reflecting nothing more than higher teaching loads and therefore less time to spend on task per course.

A more-nuanced regression analysis of the same data suggests that, although the amount of time these faculty spent planning their courses ranged widely—the interquartile range was fifty hours—those differences did not correspond to either type of institution or market. One of the more interesting general findings was that the more time a faculty member spent in advanced planning for the course, the more that same faculty member was likely to spend during the term on course preparation and even administration. The lesson seems to be that those who "wing it" in the summer do so in the fall as well.

The time that faculty spent assessing student performance followed similar patterns. On average, those who reported engaging in this activity the least were faculty at the three private Medallion research universities, followed by those at the four Good Buy/Good Opportunity institutions; again, in the latter case it was probably a function of higher teaching loads. Those who reported spending the most time assessing student performance were faculty at the two Medallion liberal arts colleges. Twenty-five percent of the faculty from the Medallion research universities reported spending less than twenty-two hours assessing the performance of their students during the term for the targeted course. The median for faculty at liberal arts colleges was sixty-five hours for the term, and 25 percent of these

Figure 3.7. Indices of Faculty Time

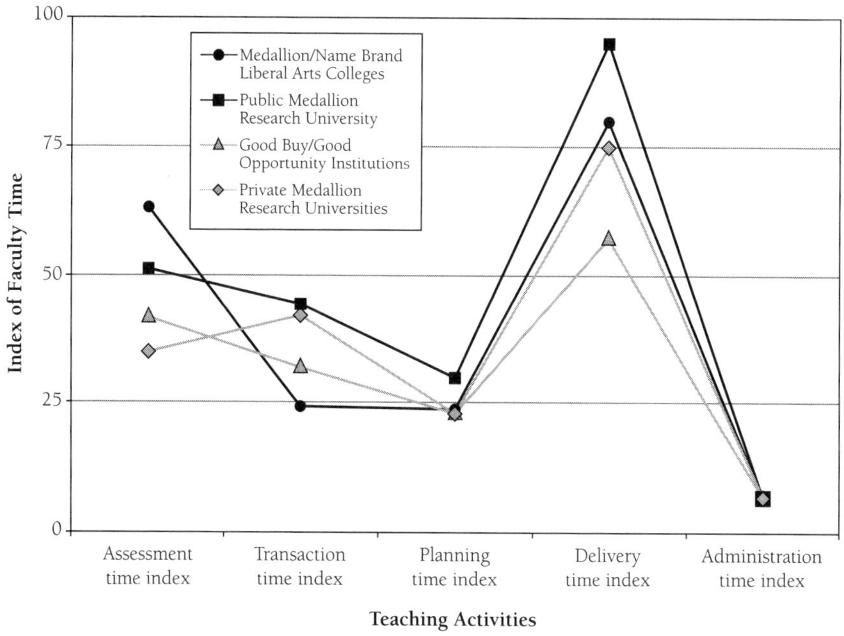

faculty reported spending more than eighty-nine hours assessing the targeted course.

When we turned to the amount of time these faculty reported spending outside of class with students enrolled in the target course, the resulting distribution was truly unexpected. On average, faculty at the Medallion research universities reported spending significantly more time (for the target course) interacting with students outside of the classroom than faculty at either of the two Medallion liberal arts colleges or at the Good Buy/Good Opportunity institutions. The explanation may be that research-based faculty are more prone to exaggeration in this respect or that liberal arts faculty are just naturally more modest. Then again, liberal arts faculty may have a more restrictive definition of what contact outside of class means than faculty at research universities. We are prepared to believe, however, that the finding is straightforward: faculty at research universities spend slightly more time per course on students outside of class, which is more likely to relate directly to their research interests and which is also likely to be part of a lower teaching load. Because the higher prices these institutions charge makes possible lower teaching loads and larger faculties (and hence, greater specialization), the higher rates of student interaction may be one important benefit that students attending research institutions receive.

The survey also focused on three content areas: technical and computer skills, communication skills, and general learning and concept skills. For each content area we constructed a composite index reflecting the average importance faculty reported attaching to each, from very important (a value of five) to not at all important (a value of one). Figure 3.8 displays the aggregate results of this analysis.

The first and most obvious conclusion we can draw from the results is that commitment to general learning is in fact a characteristic of all college courses. Commitment to this set of skills was the most widespread of all. More than half of the more than 401 interviewed faculty members rated the items within the general learning and conceptual and critical-thinking skills categories as either important or very important. In sharp contrast, only 25 percent of the sample stated the items relating to communication skills, on average, rated higher than 2.65. For technical and computer skills the 75th percentile is even lower at 1.65.

However, some apparent market ordering does exist in the data displayed in Figure 3.8. Both technical/computer skills and communication skills are consistently rated higher in the rightward group—Good Buy/Good Opportunity colleges and universities. Conversely, faculty at the four research universities rated general knowledge as being more important than did their colleagues at the other six institutions.

Amid this welter of detail are the answers to some important questions being posed of higher education, as well as an important set of insights regarding when markets do and do not matter. Do faculty at the nation's Medallion research universities teach their undergraduate courses fundamentally differently than do faculty at other institutions? Do they spend more or less time on their undergraduate courses? Do they spend more or less time with their students outside of the classroom? Do they stress different concepts or goals?

The answer is, by and large, "No." True, the private research university faculty interviewed were likely to devote less time assessing the performance of their students and spend more time outside of class interacting with students enrolled in their undergraduate courses. But those differences in themselves accounted for relatively little of the variance in how faculty allotted time to the key activities associated with teaching an undergraduate course. The more determining elements were largely disciplinary in nature, and even they related more to the skills and concepts the faculty stressed than to how they spent their time.

Somewhat to our surprise, in fact, the general pattern emerging from the data is one detailing the homogeneity of the undergraduate teaching function—a homogeneity that stretches across all institutional types and that often minimizes even disciplinary differences. Such a finding will distress those who proclaim the inherent diversity and heterogeneity of U.S. higher education. They see faculty as largely independent and autonomous, even idiosyncratic in both how and what they teach.

The larger, more obvious truth is that what one faculty member does at one institution is probably mirrored by a faculty member at a neighbor-

Figure 3.8. Skill Sets Expectation

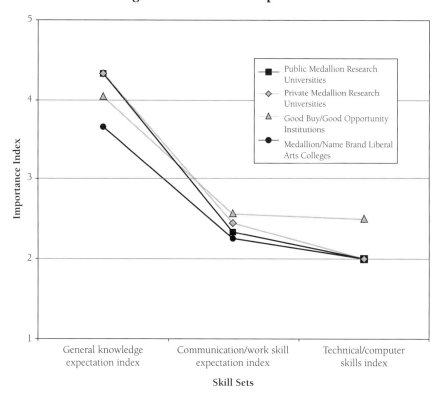

ing institution. The dominant force appears to be a faculty culture honed in graduate school that makes most members of the professorate define their obligations and responsibilities in remarkably similar ways.

Given a basically homogeneous faculty culture, it becomes even more difficult to sustain an argument that price is a function of how faculty teach. What distinguishes faculty across the nearly twelve hundred institutions for whom it is possible to calculate a market position is principally what they are paid and, we suspect, how much they are expected to teach.

What matters here is the clash between market realities and faculty culture. Given that faculty do not teach in fundamentally different ways across market segments, any differences in learning outcomes that are associated with the market will have to be attributed to causes other than curriculum and pedagogy.

4

The market can also be linked to student outcomes. This chapter traces how the Collegiate Results Instrument (CRI) measures a range of collegiate outcomes for alumni six years after graduation. Targeting alumni from institutions across the market segments, the CRI was designed to assess their values, abilities, work skills, occupations, and pursuit of lifelong learning.

Results

For educational researchers the search for reliable outcome measures has become something akin to the quest for the Holy Grail. Those who pay the bills keep asking, "What do students know? When did they learn it? Who gets credit for teaching them what they know?" For primary and secondary education answers to these questions increasingly come through the systematic and repeated testing of students, including in some cases the use of sophisticated statistical models to distribute credit and blame among teachers and schools for their students' successes and failures.

Higher education has largely escaped this testing mania. Most students see further testing as involving substantially more risk than benefit. Most faculty do not want to be evaluated—period. Still, questions remain to which both faculty and students have a real interest in finding the answers: How does one know if the educational process is working? What are college students learning? Are they learning what they really need to know? Are faculty teaching effectively? A final question ties the whole problem to the market: Does it make a difference where students enroll and how much they pay?

In the end it was the market that forced the issue of reliable outcome measures, although in an unexpected way. As students and their families paid more for their college degrees—and within the public sector, an ever-increasing share of the cost of the education they received—they began asking the question that all customers eventually pose: "How do I know I am getting my money's worth?" When organized higher education failed to provide a credible answer, *U.S. News and World Report* filled the vacuum. Thus were born the dreaded college rankings that rather than focusing on learning or other outcomes, transformed reputation and prestige into synonyms for educational quality. What the higher education market needed was a kind of *Consumer Reports*. What it got instead was a beauty contest that featured the nation's "nifty fifty," the twenty-five universities and twenty-five colleges that *U.S. News and World Report* placed in the top ranks and which get most of the media attention.

Stung by the rankings' considerable reliance on inputs (average SAT and ACT scores, average expenditures per student, admit rates, and student-faculty ratios) rather than outcomes, much of higher education renewed its quest for a valid set of measures that would also challenge the rankings' hegemony. The two most prominent of these efforts are the National Survey on Student Engagement (NSSE), funded by The Pew Charitable Trusts, and the Collegiate Results Instrument (CRI), funded by the U.S. Department of Education through its National Center on Postsecondary Improvement (NCPI).

The NSSE, as developed by George Kuh, Peter Ewell, and Russell Edgerton, focuses less on outcomes than on the processes through which most higher education institutions produce those outcomes. Growing out of a decade of activist research, much of it completed under the auspices of the American Association of Higher Education, the NSSE proceeds on the assumption that students learn best when they are engaged—with each other, with faculty, and with the communities in which they learn, work, and live. Administered principally to college seniors in their final semester, the NSSE queries respondents about their level of preparedness for class, the nature and frequency of their contact with other students and with faculty, and their work-cum-learning experiences. The NSSE then asks respondents to make two kinds of evaluations of their learning experiences: a self-estimated measure of educational gains and a judgment regarding whether they would enroll at the same undergraduate institution if they had a chance to do so again. In the spring of 2000, 225 institutions were testing the NSSE.

During roughly the same period, at the Institute for Research on Higher Education (IRHE), we completed the development and testing of our CRI. Although he bears no responsibility for our use of his insight, Morton Schapiro—then economist and dean at the University of Southern California and now economist and president at Williams College—guided the development of the CRI with a casual observation. Schapiro was part of a small research seminar convened by IRHE to think through the construction of what came to be the CRI. We had introduced the discussion by stating that what the market needed was a *Consumer Reports* for higher education. Schapiro took our suggestion literally, saying (as best we can remember): "Look, you have to find a way to do the testing. As an economist, I am not so much interested in testimony as in revealed preferences. It's the behavior that matters." We took him to mean that the educational product itself would really have to be tested. The question was how.

Part of the answer came quickly. What we really needed to know was how the graduates of a particular institution turned out: what they were like, for example, two, six, or ten years after graduation; what kinds of jobs, skills, abilities and salaries they had attained; how much further they had pursued learning after receiving their baccalaureate degrees. Although we could never know for certain the direct effects of the college they attended, we could determine if the graduates of a particular college or university could be classified in readily identifiable—that is, statistically predictable—ways.

Constructing the CRI

Three basic decisions then guided the development of the CRI. We would build it top down rather than bottom up. We would organize it around conceptual domains that included sets of "target" categories that in turn were composed of individual survey items. We would evaluate the items in the target categories together rather than treating them as valid measures in their own right.

We began with three domains. The first, Occupations, proved to be easy to specify—although, as we will make clear, income was much less informative than we had initially believed. We drew the occupational categories from a standard taxonomy used by the U.S. Bureau of Labor Statistics. Although the respondents identified their occupations from a fairly extensive list of more than eighty occupational categories, we ultimately mapped the large number of items into nine broad target categories:

• Business
• Creative arts/design
• Health/social services
• Law
• Medicine/dentistry/veterinary
• Professional (other)
• Science/engineering/technical
• Teaching/counseling
• Nonprofessional (a residual category)

The next domain, Abilities, proved more elusive. The straightforward way to uncover "abilities" is through testing. Dismissing this method as too complex and time consuming for a voluntary survey, we sought another approach. Why not present graduates with a set of tasks or problems and then ask them to "indicate how well prepared you believe you are to work on the task described." We cast the tasks as everyday scenarios that one could reasonably expect recent college graduates to encounter. In each test administration of the CRI, the respondents received ten such scenarios, developed to tap three broad target categories:

• Communicate/organize
• Quantitative
• Find information

A scenario, for example, might ask respondents to consider the following:

> Your teenage cousin is not likely to believe you when you claim that the movie *Clueless* is a modern version of the Jane Austen novel *Emma*. You want to be able to point out the major similarities in characters and plot when this young relative visits you next month.

Although completing the task in this scenario would require a number of skills, it would draw heavily on the graduates' nonquantitative analytic and research abilities. These abilities are included in the target category we named "find information."

The third domain is Work Skills. The CRI asked respondents to indicate the extent to which they were using particular skills as part of their jobs and occupations. In all, respondents were presented with twenty skill items and asked to indicate the degree to which they used them, from "Never" to "Regularly." We collected these skills into four target categories:

- Analyzing
- Writing/presenting
- Organizing
- Customer/client

The category names reflect the skills themselves. The analyzing category taps quantitative work skills; writing/presenting represents both written and oral presentations; organizing skills encompass managing and supervising people, planning, and prioritizing tasks; and the customer/client category includes a range of skills from sales to working with the elderly to working with patients.

At this point we shared a draft of the proposed CRI with Tom Erhlich, former University of Pennsylvania provost, then Indiana University president, and currently a senior scholar at the Carnegie Foundation for the Advancement of Teaching. An old friend, Erhlich not so gently complained: "There you go again, making a college education principally about jobs and work skills! What about values, lifelong learning, civic engagement?" We shared Erhlich's comments with members of a standing focus group we used to test concepts and items relating both to the CRI and the market taxonomy, and they agreed. The result was the addition of two domains: Lifelong Learning and Personal Values.

The measure of Lifelong Learning captures the respondents' pursuit of postbaccalaureate educational experiences, as well as their attitudes and intentions regarding learning. The target categories in this domain include the following:

- Courses/certificates /credentials
- Advanced degrees
- Keep informed
- Like to learn

The keep informed category subsumes items related to keeping abreast of such fields as science, economics, and current events; like to learn relates to curiosity about the scenarios used in the abilities domain.

Completing the CRI, the Personal Values domain includes the following target categories:

- Civic/community
- Arts and culture
- Religious
- Physical fitness

Again, the names of the categories reflect the values being queried. The civic/community category includes political participation and community service (participating in volunteer work, working on political campaigns, working for social causes, etc.). The arts and culture category includes both participating in and being a part of an audience for a wide range of cultural and artistic activities. The religious category refers to formal religious activities and does not include activities such as meditation and spirituality. Physical fitness includes both individual activities and participation in team sports. For each of the categories in the Personal Values domain, we combined survey items reflecting attitudes (for example, the importance the respondent attached to participating in volunteer work) with items that tracked the respondents' self-reported activity (for example, how often the respondent performed volunteer work).

Following our top-down approach, we started with our set of five domains for which we then drafted individual survey items within each category. In turn, we tested those items using panels of graduate students enrolled in University of Pennsylvania's higher education program. We included items that passed this phase in the first-round alpha testing of the CRI in 1998, which involved approximately two hundred randomly selected 1992 graduates from fifteen institutions, all members of the Knight Higher Education Collaborative. The alpha test provided just under fourteen hundred usable CRIs. Our analysis of this pilot set allowed us to hone the items, remap them to particular domain categories, and revise our thinking, for example, about the usefulness of the income question.

The second, or beta, test of the CRI used similar procedures but a substantially larger test population: more than 112,000 valid mailings yielding over 38,500 respondents from eighty institutions belonging to the Knight Higher Education Collaborative. (About 33,800 responses were from alumni in the core set of 1991–1994 graduates; an additional 4,700 were returned by other alumni who were included in the same institutions' mailings to enable those institutions to analyze similarities and differences across classes.) Unsuccessful items in the first instrument led to changes in the survey. For example, we revised some of the ten scenarios. We also included an expanded set of activities on which respondents reported and revised the income bands, while remaining skeptical about the usefulness of the item itself.

In the analysis of both the alpha and beta administrations, we tested our a priori assignment of specific item sets to particular categories within the domains. Applying a discriminant analysis to the survey, we sought to see how the items clustered post facto. The results validated our initial construct for all but a few items. For example, we simply dropped from the analysis two of the twenty items in the work skills domain.

The final result was the CRI presented in Exhibit 4.1, a four-page instrument that most respondents were able to complete in less than twenty minutes. The version presented in Exhibit 4.1 includes our internal alphanumeric identifiers (not printed on the administered CRI) used to enumerate how the individual items were combined to create twenty-three target categories. (We omitted the residual category nonprofessional from our initial Occupations domain list.)

Missing from the final list of domains and categories is respondents' reported income six years after college graduation. Although the data collected on income appeared to be reasonable, income itself was problematic because it was clearly a function of both occupation and longevity in that occupation. If we knew the respondent's occupation, we could predict with reasonable accuracy his or her income. However, we also knew that physicians, for example, who were usually in a residency six years after college graduation, were reporting incomes well below their likely earnings just a few years hence.

After drafting and subsequently finalizing the instruments, we deliberated on the particular group of alumni to survey. Should it be recent graduates fresh out of college? Older alumni who had settled into their careers and lifestyles? Ultimately, for both pragmatic and conceptual reasons, we settled on alumni six years after graduation. Alumni six years out would likely have settled into some initial career path, would have most likely at least enrolled in postbaccalaureate education if that goal was to be pursued at all, and would have crystallized some of their values and abilities. At the same time, many of the alumni would have maintained sufficient contact with their alma maters so that their mailing addresses would be valid.

Scoring the CRI

The analytic goal of the CRI is to derive an institutional portrait or signature of an institution as reflected in the postgraduation experiences of recent alumni. We could then readily compare that portrait or signature with those of other colleges and universities. The device we used to cast these signatures was a set of target scores, one for each of the twenty-three target categories. The target scores represent the proportion of an institution's respondents who achieved a particular composite score in each of the target categories.

We scored the individual items that composed a target category by assigning ordinal values to the responses. For example, the items that make up the

Exhibit 4.1. The Collegiate Results Instrument

SECTION I   Your Current Job and Educational Activities
1. What are your current work, school, and other responsibilities? Fill in **all** circles that apply.

Employment for Pay		Other Activities	
Work full-time (FT) only	O	Attend school FT	O
Work part-time (PT) only	O	Attend school PT	O
Work FT and PT at more than one job	O	Work as a volunteer	O
Work PT at more than one job	O	Keep house	O
In the military (FT)	O	Child or elder care	O
Looking for work	O		

2. If you have sought additional schooling since your bachelor's degree, please fill in **all** the circles that apply.

	Completed since my BA/BS	Currently enrolled in or working toward (either PT or FT)
Certificate or Diploma	O	O
Professional Degree (*Law, Medicine, Dentistry, Veterinary Medicine*)	O	O
MBA	O	O
Master's (*not* MBA)	O	O
Doctorate	O	O
Additional BA/BS	O	O
Non-Degree Courses	O	O

> If you **have not been in the workforce**
> since earning your bachelor's degree, skip ahead to **Question 8.**

3. From **Table A** enclosed, enter the code that most closely describes your occupation in this box: Then, please transcribe your occupation code by filling in the appropriate circles below.

	1	2	3	4	5	6	7	8	9
First Digit	O	O	O	O	O	O	O	O	O
Second Digit	O	O	O	O	O	O	O	O	O

4. Below is a set of skills and activities you may use or perform in your current job/position. Please fill in the circle under the category that **best indicates** the extent to which you actually use each skill or engage in each activity in your current job/position.

I use this skill or engage in this activity	Never	Occasionally	Regularly
A Retrieve information	O	O	O
B Manage/supervise people	O	O	O
C Plan projects/events	O	O	O
D Write reports or manuals	O	O	O
E Set priorities among competing tasks	O	O	O
F Make presentations	O	O	O
G Interpret data	O	O	O
H Work with technical equipment	O	O	O
I Work with budgets/financial records/accounts	O	O	O

Exhibit 4.1. (*continued*)

I use this skill or engage in this activity	Never	Occasionally	Regularly
J Diagnose problems	O	O	O
K Work with the elderly	O	O	O
L Design products/procedures/performances	O	O	O
M Set agenda for meetings	O	O	O
N Write for publication	O	O	O
O Work with clients/customers/patients	O	O	O
P Perform statistical analyses	O	O	O
Q Sell products/services	O	O	O
R Work with children	O	O	O
S Perform in public	O	O	O
T Read professional journals/periodicals	O	O	O

5. The list below includes many of the academic content areas studied in college. Please indicate whether you draw on these subjects in your current job/ position, and whether you ever took **any** courses in the specific area during college.

	I use this subject in my job/position		I took at least one course in college	
	Yes	No	Yes	No
Business	O	O	O	O
Communications	O	O	O	O
Composition/Writing	O	O	O	O
Computer Science	O	O	O	O
Education	O	O	O	O
Engineering	O	O	O	O
Foreign Languages	O	O	O	O
Health Sciences	O	O	O	O
Humanities	O	O	O	O
Mathematics/Statistics	O	O	O	O
Natural/Physical Sciences	O	O	O	O
Social Sciences	O	O	O	O
Social Work/Services	O	O	O	O
Visual/Performing/Design Arts	O	O	O	O

6. How closely is your current job/position related to your major field of study in college? Fill in the appropriate circle below.

Directly Related (*Uses specific skills and knowledge of the major*)   O
Indirectly Related (*Draws on general knowledge but not specific skills of the major*)   O
Unrelated (*Does not draw on knowledge acquired as part of the major*)   O

7. Please fill in the circle that best approximates your annual earnings for this current tax year.

Less than $15,000	O	$40,001-$45,000	O
$15,001-$20,000	O	$45,001-$50,000	O
$20,001-$25,000	O	$50,001-$55,000	O
$25,001-$30,000	O	$55,001-$60,000	O
$30,001-$35,000	O	Over $60,000	O
$35,001-$40,000	O		

Exhibit 4.1. (*continued*)

Section II   Your Personal Preferences

8. Below is a set of items related to your personal values. Using a scale of 1 to 5, please indicate how important each item is to your satisfaction in life by filling in the appropriate circle (1 = Not at all important; 5 = Very important).

	Importance to my personal well-being				
	Not at all important ⟵			⟶ Very important	
	1	2	3	4	5
A Forming and retaining friendships	O	O	O	O	O
B Enjoying artistic experiences	O	O	O	O	O
C Keeping informed about local and national politics	O	O	O	O	O
D Spending time with family	O	O	O	O	O
E Having financial security	O	O	O	O	O
F Working for a political or social cause	O	O	O	O	O
G Being physically fit	O	O	O	O	O
H Participating in volunteer work	O	O	O	O	O
I Engaging in religious observance	O	O	O	O	O
J Participating in sports	O	O	O	O	O
K Achieving personal wealth	O	O	O	O	O
L Keeping current about scientific developments	O	O	O	O	O

9. Please review the list of activities below and indicate how often you participated in each activity during the last year by filling in the appropriate circle.

During the past year, I	Never	Occasionally	Regularly
A Participated in team sports	O	O	O
B Performed volunteer work	O	O	O
C Went to the movies	O	O	O
D Attended or hosted social gatherings	O	O	O
E Attended religious services	O	O	O
F Attended meetings of organizations centered on a personal interest	O	O	O
G Read religious works	O	O	O
H Engaged in arts and crafts	O	O	O
I Attended live concerts or theatrical events	O	O	O
J Took courses	O	O	O
K Visited art galleries or museums	O	O	O
L Jogged, biked, swam, skated, skied, or worked out	O	O	O
M Read novels for pleasure	O	O	O
N Read about the economy or stock market	O	O	O
O Read about scientific issues	O	O	O
P Read about international events	O	O	O
Q Used the Internet to gather information	O	O	O
R Worked in a political campaign	O	O	O

	Yes	No
I traveled outside the U.S. in the last 12 months.	O	O
I voted in the 1996 presidential election.	O	O

Exhibit 4.1. (*continued*)

SECTION III   Your Personal and Academic Information

10. Please provide the personal and academic information requested below by filling in the appropriate circle.

Your age:

Under	25 O	28 O	32 O	36 to 40 O
	25 O	29 O	33 O	41 to 45 O
	26 O	30 O	34 O	46 to 50 O
	27 O	31 O	35 O	Over 50 O

Your gender   Male O   Female O

Your ethnicity (fill in **all** that apply):

White, Non-Hispanic O   Hispanic Origin   O   Asian or Pacific Islander   O
African American/Black O   American Indian or Alaskan Native   O
Other _____   O

Your citizenship: Are you a U.S. citizen?   Yes O   No O

In what year did you receive your
bachelor's degree?

Before	1988 O	1991 O	1995 O
	1988 O	1992 O	1996 O
	1989 O	1993 O	1997 O
	1990 O	1994 O	

In what year did you **first enroll** in a degree program in **any** college
(two- or four-year; PT or FT)?

Before	1980 O	1984 O	1989 O
	1980 O	1985 O	1990 O
	1981 O	1986 O	1991 O
	1982 O	1987 O	1992 O
	1983 O	1988 O	1993 or later O

Please indicate the area in which you **majored in college**. If you majored in more than one area, fill in **all** that apply.

Business	O	Humanities	O
Communications	O	Mathematics/Statistics	O
Composition/Writing	O	Natural/Physical Sciences	O
Computer Science	O	Social Sciences	O
Education	O	Social Work/Services	O
Engineering	O	Visual/Performing/Design Arts	O
Foreign Languages	O	Other _____	O
Health Sciences	O		

SECTION IV   Preparation

11. In the table below, you will find 10 scenarios—situations, tasks, or problems that might need to be researched, solved, and/or performed in the workplace or in life.

After reading **each scenario**, indicate in **Part I** how well prepared you believe you are to work on the task described. Fill in the appropriate circle, using a scale of 1 to 5 (1 = Not at all prepared; 5 = Very well prepared). Then, in **Part II**, indicate whether or not you would like to learn more about the task by filling in the circle under Yes or No in the column, "I'd like to learn more about this."

Exhibit 4.1. (*continued*)

Scenarios	Part I Not at all ← → well prepared					Part II I'd like to learn more about this.	
	1	2	3	4	5	Yes	No
You are part of a four-person team that has been conducting research for the past month to put together a set of talking points for your boss's presentation to a major client. Your boss has just had a skiing accident and is unable to make the presentation. You are asked to do it instead. A	O	O	O	O	O	O	O
You have a friend who is breeding a pair of sheepdogs. She already has a commitment from a buyer who wants four female puppies. Her breeder's manual includes a chart showing the probabilities of bearing litters of various sizes. You are asked to help her figure out how likely it is that at least four females will be born in the first litter. B	O	O	O	O	O	O	O
You have heard about an experimental drug to reduce high cholesterol. A friend who is suffering from this condition asks you to help him find information about the known efficacy and safety of the drug. C	O	O	O	O	O	O	O
Your firm, which employed 15 people when you began working there, recently expanded to include nearly 100 employees. You are asked to prepare a training manual describing office and personnel procedures based on practices you helped to establish. D	O	O	O	O	O	O	O
Population shifts necessitate closing two branch offices of the bank for which you work and opening three new offices. All staff will be reassigned from the old offices to the new ones. You are asked to develop a comprehensive plan for the staff transition process. E	O	O	O	O	O	O	O
The building you live in has been converted to a condominium. You were about to sign a three-year rental renewal lease. Now, you must decide whether to purchase your apartment, based on the financial implications of the rental purchase decision. F	O	O	O	O	O	O	O
Your teenage cousin is not likely to believe you when you claim that the movie *Clueless* is a modern version of the Jane Austen novel *Emma*. You want to be able to point out the major similarities in characters and plot when this young relative visits you next month. G	O	O	O	O	O	O	O

Exhibit 4.1. (*continued*)

Scenarios	Part I: Not at all ←→ Very well prepared					Part II: I'd like to learn more about this.	
	1	2	3	4	5	Yes	No
Your firm values positive employee morale. Consequently, it offers a variety of benefits and services to all its employees. Recently, employee morale has declined dramatically and new employee recruitment has dropped off significantly. You are asked to uncover what is causing the problem. **H**	O	O	O	O	O	O	O
Your employer provides a college tuition benefit for dependent children that is equivalent to full tuition at State University. A colleague has been offered a job by another company, which does not provide this benefit. She has asked you to help her calculate the increased salary she would require to recover the loss of the benefit for her one child who is planning to begin college in 4 years. **I**	O	O	O	O	O	O	O
You work for a national chain of bookstores that is considering opening a store abroad. Significant business practices would have to be altered (e.g., selecting a market-sensitive stock of books). Your task is to collect enough information about the country's culture in general and the people's reading habits in particular to advise your company with confidence. **J**	O	O	O	O	O	O	O

target categories in the Work Skills domain derive from CRI Question 4 (see Exhibit 4.1). Those items were scored as follows: "Never" = 0; "Occasionally" = 1; "Regularly" = 2. For each respondent we computed an index (a composite score that equaled the sum of the scores for all items in a target category) and then compared that index to a threshold value.

We usually set the threshold at the middle value—the value that would have been attained had the respondent scored "1" on each item in a target category. For example, the organizing category consists of five items in Question 4. A respondent could achieve a composite score ranging from zero (responding "Never" to all five items) up to ten (responding "Regularly" to all five items) or any value in between. With the threshold value set to five, an institution's target score represents the proportion of respondents whose composite score was greater than five. We believe that a respondent's score that exceeded the threshold indicates that he or she was strongly inclined to use the skills (or hold the values, abilities, and other characteristics) defined for that particular target category.

The analytic task, resulting in an institutional target score, thus became a matter of five simple steps. Figure 4.1 provides an overview of our scoring methodology.

1. Group the individual items into their respective target categories.
2. Calculate a composite score for each alumnus for each target category.
3. Determine whether each individual respondent had exceeded the threshold value for each target category.
4. Assign each respondent a weight based on gender, ethnicity, and reported major to correct for response bias.
5. Determine the (weighted) proportion of each institution's respondents that had exceeded the threshold value for each target category.

The appendix includes a map of the CRI terrain, which displays the assignment of individual items to target categories within our five conceptual domains. Notice that the Personal Values domain includes items that were evaluated by respondents as "Never," "Occasionally," or "Regularly" (Questions 4 and 9 in Exhibit 4.1), which we scored on a three-point scale (zero to two). We also included items that were evaluated on a five-point scale from "Not At All Important" to "Very Important" (Question 8 in Exhibit 4.1). We debated how to combine these two disparate scales while giving equal weight to items in both scoring systems. We posited a series of solutions and performed some sensitivity testing to see if the different schemes produced wildly different results. Ultimately, we were satisfied with the solution that reduced the five-point scale to a three-point scale by combining the two left-hand scores in Question 8 (into zero), assigning the middle to its own category (one), and combining the two right-hand scores (into two).

Response Rates

We were a bit surprised and more than a little heartened by the substantial response rate of those who were asked by their institutions to complete a CRI. In the 1998 test, which involved fifteen institutions and random samples of 1992 graduates, the overall response rate was 40 percent while the response rates for individual institutions ranged from a low of 21 percent to a high of 69 percent. In the 1999 test, which involved eighty institutions, response rates again varied widely—from under 20 percent to over 70 percent. CRIs were mailed to just under 118,000 alumni, predominantly 1993 graduates. Based on institutional reports, we estimate that between five thousand and six thousand were undeliverable. The total return of completed and usable CRIs for this study was 38,560, yielding an overall response rate of 34.2 percent.

Figure 4.1. An Overview of the CRI Target Score Analysis

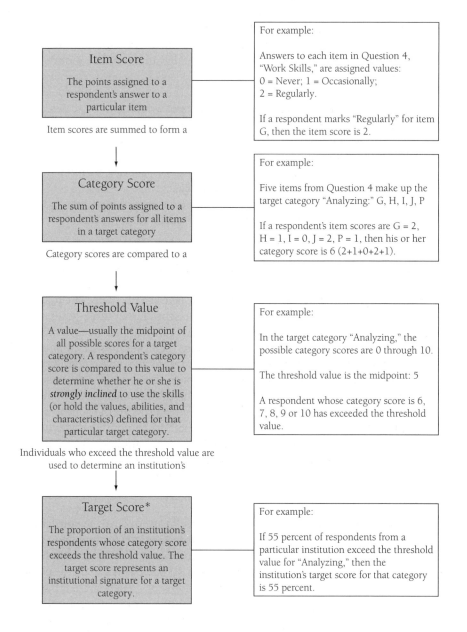

Item Score

The points assigned to a respondent's answer to a particular item

Item scores are summed to form a

For example:

Answers to each item in Question 4, "Work Skills," are assigned values: 0 = Never; 1 = Occasionally; 2 = Regularly.

If a respondent marks "Regularly" for item G, then the item score is 2.

Category Score

The sum of points assigned to a respondent's answers for all items in a target category

Category scores are compared to a

For example:

Five items from Question 4 make up the target category "Analyzing:" G, H, I, J, P

If a respondent's item scores are G = 2, H = 1, I = 0, J = 2, P = 1, then his or her category score is 6 (2+1+0+2+1).

Threshold Value

A value—usually the midpoint of all possible scores for a target category. A respondent's category score is compared to this value to determine whether he or she is *strongly inclined* to use the skills (or hold the values, abilities, and characteristics) defined for that particular target category.

Individuals who exceed the threshold value are used to determine an institution's

For example:

In the target category "Analyzing," the possible category scores are 0 through 10.

The threshold value is the midpoint: 5

A respondent whose category score is 6, 7, 8, 9 or 10 has exceeded the threshold value.

Target Score*

The proportion of an institution's respondents whose category score exceeds the threshold value. The target score represents an institutional signature for a target category.

For example:

If 55 percent of respondents from a particular institution exceed the threshold value for "Analyzing," then the institution's target score for that category is 55 percent.

* Occupation and postbaccalaureate education are not scored using indices. Rather, the target score is the percentage of respondents whose occupations or educational attainment fit the particular criteria.

In the alpha test of the CRI institutional response, rates varied by market segment and control. That trend proved to be the case in the 1999 test of the CRI as well. Table 4.1 shows the average response rates by market segment (Medallion, Name Brand, Good Buy, Good Opportunity, User-Friendly/Convenience).

We believe these differences reflect in part the diligence as well as the eagerness with which some institutions track their alumni. The highest response rates were for the Medallion and Name Brand institutions in the set—colleges and universities that have proved remarkably successful at raising funds from their graduates. We suspect that the type of student recruited and enrolled plays a role as well. Graduates of Medallion and Name Brand institutions were the most likely to attend one—and only one—undergraduate institution and to graduate in five years or less. Institutional climate and scale also play a role, however. The statistic not revealed in Table 4.1 is that liberal arts colleges, regardless of market segment, had substantially higher response rates than any other institutions in the survey. In the pilot the top response rate was nearly 70 percent, with three institutions following with response rates in excess of 50 percent. All four institutions are small, enrolling fewer than three thousand students; three of the four are liberal arts colleges, suggesting that the intensity of student engagement, for which they seek and advertise, pays off in that their graduates remain connected to their alma maters.

The finding was repeated in the larger study. All but one of the institutions with a response rate over 50 percent were small colleges whose enrollments ranged from under seven hundred to nearly twenty-one hundred. The exception was a large research university. However, that institution decided to mail surveys to alumni of its honors college only, a select group of students who in effect attended a "small liberal arts college" within the university.

In general, the response rates on individual items across the CRI were remarkably high. If a graduate returned the CRI, he or she took the time to answer all of the questions. This thoroughness applied even for the scenarios,

Table 4.1. Response Rate for Eighty CRI Institutions in the 1999 Beta Administration by Market Segment and Control

Market Segment	Public	Private
User Friendly/Convenience	27.3%	NA*
Good Opportunity	28.2%	30.0%
Good Buy	29.0%	32.7%
Name Brand	—	38.9%
Name Brand/Medallion	36.6%	
Medallion	—	42.1%

*NA = not applicable.

which come at the end of the CRI and involve reading ten paragraphs. Although a small increase in omissions occurred toward the last few of the ten, the completion rate never dropped below 98.5 percent.

Response Bias

In the alpha administration we collected student record data for the entire group of 1992 graduates from the fifteen participating institutions, thus enabling us to examine how well those who returned a completed CRI compared to all recipients of the baccalaureate degree in that year. We compared gender, ethnicity, age, major, entering status (freshman versus transfer), and grades. The results, shown in Table 4.2, indicate that for most institutions and for most variables, the respondents exhibited enough similarity to the graduating class that statistical differences were not detected. Only for the last institution, the public Name Brand university that sampled the graduates of only one of its undergraduate schools, were consistent differences evident—as would be expected.

Interestingly, in only one of the remaining fourteen institutions were the grade point averages (GPAs) of responding graduates significantly higher than those of the 1992 graduates as a whole. The intuition of most observers might suggest that the more successful students are more likely to respond to alumni surveys. Because the only income data available to use comes from the CRI itself, we have no way of formally testing whether, for example, graduates with higher incomes were more likely to respond. We can say, however, based on the 1998 test and analysis, that students who were more or less successful in terms of their GPAs did not appear to be more or less likely to complete the CRI.

We did not collect the student data from the beta institutions. Instead, we used publicly available data submitted by the eighty institutions to the U.S. Department of Education through the IPEDS reporting protocol to estimate the distribution of graduates by major, gender, and ethnicity. We compared those distributions of all graduates to the distribution of CRI respondents for the same key variables. Tables 4.3 and 4.4 show the expected and actual percentages for these attributes. We also used the IPEDS data to calculate the weights correcting for response bias when reporting CRI results on an institutional level.

Finally, we compared the distribution of occupations reported by the CRI's core respondents (graduates between 1991 and 1994) with the national distribution of occupations for college graduates aged twenty-seven to thirty as reflected in the U.S. Bureau of Labor Statistics' Current Population Surveys. We did not anticipate the close fit between the two distributions because we had not recruited a random sample of institutions for the study (see Figure 4.2). Nevertheless, we now have reason to believe that the core 33,800-plus respondents to the 1999 administration of the CRI constitute a fairly representative sample of recent college graduates.

Table 4.2. Comparison of CRI Respondents and Their Graduating Classes:
Demographic and Academic Characteristics of Fifteen Institutions (1998 Alpha Administration)

Institution	Gender	Ethnicity	Age	Major	Transfer Status	Grade Point Average	Variables Tested	Number with Significant Difference	Percentage Not Significant
A	no	no	no	no	no	no	6	0	100
B	no	no	no	no	no	no	6	0	100
C	yes*	no	no	no	no	no	6	0	100
D	no	no	no	no	no	no	6	0	100
F	no	no	no	no	no	no	6	0	100
G	no	—	no	no	no	no	5	0	100
H	—	—	no	no	no	no	4	0	100
J	no	no	no	yes**	no	no	6	1	83
K	no	no	yes*	no	no	no	6	1	83
L	—	—	yes**	no	no	no	4	1	75
M	no	yes**	no	no	no	yes*	6	2	67
N	yes	no	yes	no	no	no	6	2	67
P	yes**	no	no	yes**	no	no	6	2	67
Q	no	yes**	yes**	no	—	no	5	2	60
R***	no	no	yes*	yes**	yes**	yes**	6	4	33

*Significant at p < .05.

**Significant at p < .01.

***Sample selected from a special subpopulation in one school.

Note: "Yes" = significant difference between respondents and universe.

Table 4.3. Distribution of Graduates by Gender and Ethnicity: All Graduates Versus CRI Respondents (1999 Beta Administration)

	Percentage of All Graduates (Expected)*	Percentage of CRI Respondents (Actual)
Gender		
Female	51.9	56.8
Male	48.1	43.2
Ethnicity		
African American	3.9	2.5
Native American	0.4	0.3
Asian	5.4	3.2
Hispanic	3.3	2.6
White	81.6	88.0
All other	5.4	3.4

*From IPEDS completions reports for the appropriate years

Table 4.4. Distribution of Graduates by Major: All Graduates Versus CRI Respondents (1999 Beta Administration)

Majors	Percentage of All Graduates (Expected)*	Percentage of CRI Respondents (Actual)
Business	19.2	16.9
Communications	5.1	4.9
Computer science	2.3	2.2
Engineering	9.7	9.7
Education	7.1	7.7
Foreign languages	1.4	2.4
Humanities (English, philosophy, religion)	6.1	8.8
Health sciences	5.6	7.0
Social sciences	24.8	16.6
Math/statistics	1.4	2.0
Social work/services	0.7	1.9
Natural/physical sciences	5.9	8.3
Visual/performing/design arts	4.9	5.6
Other	5.9	6.1

*From IPEDS completions reports for the appropriate years.

Conducting the study in two successive years allowed us to test the reliability of the CRI. Our primary question was whether an institution's alumni would respond differently to identical items in different administrations of the CRI. Selecting the six institutions that participated in both the 1998 and 1999 CRI studies, we examined the patterns of institutional responses, focusing our analysis on the Abilities domain because the items in its categories, the scenarios, represented the most complex questions in the CRI. We had purposefully included four scenarios in both the alpha and beta instrument (see Exhibit 4.1, Question 11, Scenarios A, F, G, and J). We

Figure 4.2. Occupations of CRI Core Respondents (Bachelor's Degree, 1991–1994) Compared with National Occupation Norms for Twenty-Seven- to Thirty-Year-Olds

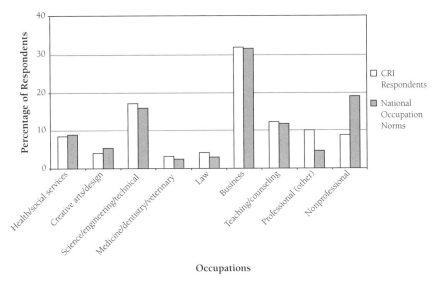

Occupations

found for one scenario (F) no statistical difference (p < .05 in all cases) in the responses between years at any of the six repeating institutions. Each of the other three scenarios (A, G, and J) showed a statistically significant difference in response patterns for just one specific institution (at p < .01). We expected this result: the institution with the changing response patterns used a different sampling strategy in each year. A major research university, it drew its sample from one particular college for the alpha study but sampled across the whole university for the second round. The five institutions using the same sampling rules for both years derived reliably consistent results from the CRI. Figure 4.3 illustrates the responses to Scenario J by the institution that changed its sampling procedure and by one institution that did not.

With these results in hand, we turn next to what the CRI can tell institutions about the choices they face as they build programs of undergraduate education and about the choices student shoppers face as they decide where to apply and then to enroll.

Figure 4.3. Responses to Scenario J by Alumni
at Two Institutions (1998 and 1999)

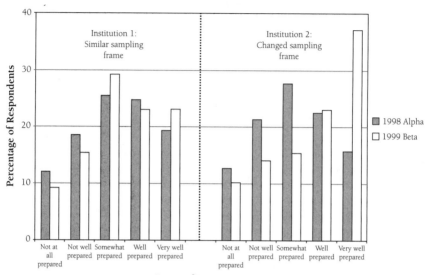

5

This chapter describes how the Collegiate Results Instrument (CRI) became a tool for helping high school juniors and seniors make better-informed college choices. The CRI serves as the underlying logic used by bestcollegepicks.com, a Peterson's Web engine, to match student aspirations and preferences with likely alumni outcomes to yield a list of institutions in which the student shopper might want to enroll.

Choices

The maxim "Demand rather than cost sets price" is the first tenet of market analysis. The second—and for our purposes, more intriguing—axiom is "In markets, the range as well as the quality of products is a function of the skill that consumers exercise as knowing shoppers." Much of the dysfunction in today's educational market derives from the fact that most educational consumers are not well-informed shoppers. They are too quick to mistake prestige for quality, too little aware of their own important role in the educational transaction, and too seldom able to balance short-term convenience against long-term return.

One of the lessons businesses have learned in this age of consumerism is that they have a fundamental stake in creating good shoppers—buyers who both know what they want and are prepared to make their purchases based on price and known quality. In the 1980s Ford Motor Company rebuilt its market position in part by making this lesson the linchpin of its marketing strategy and slogan, "Quality is Job One!" Ford's message to its employees was simple: produce a quality product, and your fortunes will rise. The message to consumers was more subtle but otherwise equally direct: when you educate yourself about quality, you will want to buy a Ford. In its ongoing series of commercials and advertisements, Ford indeed taught the public what to expect in a quality automobile.

Ford's strategy was buttressed by the growth of a quality measures industry that provided external validation to individual claims of quality. The two best known and most successful of these external monitors are J. D. Power and Associates, which regularly and consistently measures customer satisfaction, and Consumers Union, whose well-known and well-regarded publication *Consumer Reports* tests and rates consumer products. In both cases the would-be consumer had at his or her disposal a ready comparison of products. Just as important, the industries that manufactured those products have access to the same information about the quality of their products and by extrapolation, the measures of quality that were proving important to the buying public.

Closing the Loop for Higher Education

In the language of quality assurance this linking of consumer and producer is called a "positive feedback loop." The producer receives feedback about what the consumer wants and is prepared to pay for, and the consumer benefits through the development of a range of products that closely resemble his or her preferences. What makes the loop work is good information—about consumer choices on the one hand and measures of product quality on the other.

From the outset we intended the CRI to provide precisely that kind of positive feedback loop for higher education, by giving both consumers and institutions a reliable set of measures on the nature of the educational experiences individual colleges and universities provide. We wanted student and parent consumers to make more informed choices, and we wanted colleges and universities to make better investments in both the scope and quality of their educational programs. For the CRI to provide this linkage, we knew we would have to satisfy three conditions:

1. We would have to be able to generalize the CRI's initial results so they could apply to most of the institutions competing in the market for undergraduate education.
2. We would have to make those results broadly and readily available to college-bound high school seniors in terms that helped them develop meaningful college choices.
3. We would have to develop a set of measures and reports that enabled collegiate communities—faculty, students, administrators, and trustees—to make meaningful program choices from discussions that compared what they wanted to accomplish with what they were in fact accomplishing.

The remainder of this chapter describes how we took up each of these challenges, beginning with how we reported the results of the 1999 test of the CRI to the eighty institutions that participated in the survey.

Institutional Reports

One of the tyrannies imposed by institutional rankings is the importance they lend to scorekeeping—higher education institutions want to know not just how good they are but which of their peers they best in head-to-head competition. At one time only admissions officers kept score; now everyone does, aided by the very public presentation of "America's Best Colleges" or similar ranking schemes.

We understand that the CRI makes possible further win-lose comparisons, although we have done our best to minimize the likelihood that it would result in another ranking system. In part, we did so by using standards against which all institutions could be compared. Thus for any given target category, every institution could prove a winner if it had a high target score—if most of its graduates exceeded the threshold value for that particular category.

We also tried to reduce the value of the CRI as a winner-take-all ranking system by developing a wide range of target categories. Our presumption, borne out in each test of the CRI, was that institutions would prove to be winners in some categories but not in all—although one could still count the number of categories in which an institution scored at or near the top. The overall result, however, was as we had hoped. The eighty institutions looked quite different from one another not only across but within market segments. Most institutions, it turned out, had readily identifiable signatures.

To capture those differences we developed a reporting system that displayed a target score for each institution in each of the CRI's twenty-three target categories. We then color coded these scores, drawing on the circular rings of a bull's-eye target: a red bull's-eye at the center indicating that two-thirds of that institution's graduates exceeded the threshold value for that category; a middle ring in yellow signaling that a majority but less than two-thirds of an institution's graduates exceeded the threshold value; and a blue outer ring indicating that less than half of an institution's graduates exceeded the threshold value for that category.

With the exception of the Occupations and Lifelong Learning domains, the target score indicates the point at which the respondent is said to be strongly inclined to exhibit that value, ability, work skill, or educational perspective. Hence, in the most direct interpretation of the color codes, red indicates that 66.7 percent or more of the institution's graduates were strongly inclined, yellow indicates that between 50 and 66.7 percent were strongly inclined, and blue indicates that less than one-half of the institution's graduates were strongly inclined.

The interpretation of the color-coded target scores for Occupations and Lifelong Learning follow a similar path, but the threshold values are based on the national mean for that occupation or level of subsequent education: red indicates that the percentage of an institution's graduates in that occupational or educational category exceeded the national norm by at least 50 percent, yellow indicates that the percentage of the institution's graduates exceeded the national norm (for institutions not receiving red), and blue indicates that the percentage was less than the national norm. The national norms derived from the U.S. Bureau of Labor Statistics survey data and were based on adults with at least a college education and aged twenty-seven to thirty.

The best way to interpret the CRI results, we told participating institutions, was to compare their expectations against our findings. Thus the documentation we sent to the institutions advised the reader to proceed in the following manner:

> [E]xamine the institutional profile, as a whole, and . . . compare that profile to your expectations based on your institutional culture, curriculum, and co-curriculum. For example, if you emphasize written and oral communication in your programs, you might expect high scores on the 'Communicate/ Organize' Target score in the Ability section. If you require community service, then you would expect that ethos to carry forward among your alumni. If you have a specialized curriculum, your alumni will likely be drawn to particular fields and will use particular skills. If yours is a multifaceted institution, then you might expect to see moderate scores across many Target indices, rather than spikes of strength in some areas.

The power of the CRI reports lies in their ability to let an institution see itself as a whole. And the most accessible part of that portrait resides in the two sets of graphs that allow an institution to see at a glance where its graduates were and just as important, where they were not.

We were struck by just how unique the signatures of the participating institutions proved to be. As we laid out the separate graphs on the IRHE's library table, the subtle and often not-so-subtle differences the graphs revealed became clear. In time we came to focus on four liberal arts colleges, each part of the Medallion market segment, each known to be a direct competitor of at least two of the other four, and each fiercely proud of its signature in the marketplace.

These institutions—all coeducational—are about the same size, graduating from just over 400 to approximately 550 students per year. They all practice selective admissions, enroll nearly all their undergraduates on a full-time basis, charge high tuition, and provide healthy financial aid to offset student costs. Although they are located in a variety of geographic regions—New England, the Middle Atlantic, and the Midwest—all enjoy sylvan settings in rural towns or moderately sized cities.

In general, the liberal arts colleges had come to play a special role in the CRI project. Almost uniformly, liberal arts colleges had higher response rates, regardless of market segment. Among the four liberal arts colleges on which we focused, the highest CRI response rate exceeded 71 percent, followed by response rates of 54.5 percent, 50.5 percent, and finally, a respectable but disappointing 39 percent. We found that what liberal arts colleges have historically argued on their own behalf is in fact the case: something about the experience of being educated at a small residential college with a curriculum well focused on the liberal arts bonded the graduates of these institutions to their alma maters in enduring ways. Those who pursued baccalaureate education at these colleges, for whatever reason, stuck with their alma maters better than any other identifiable group within the sample of respondents.

What did the CRI specifically tell us about the graduates of these institutions? The best place to start is with the graph that mapped the CRI's Personal Values, Abilities, Work Skills, and Lifelong Learning domains (we discuss two Lifelong Learning domains—advanced degrees and courses, certificates, and credentials—under postbaccalaureate education). For the purposes of this demonstration, we labeled these institutions Colleges A, B, C, and D. This exercise also gives us a chance to introduce the CRI's basic reporting format, in which we have transformed the bull's-eye into a set of bar charts.

Figure 5.1 is a straightforward graphic representation of College A's target scores along the thirteen indices for which exceeding the threshold value indicates that the respondent was strongly inclined to exhibit that attribute. (A set of color presentations of the figures in this chapter can be found on the National Center for Postsecondary Improvement's Web site, ncpi.stanford.edu.) The display summarizes the weighted results for College A as a whole, telling us what percentage of the weighted sample exceeded the threshold on each of the thirteen indices. Where the bar is dark gray, we know that more than two-thirds of the weighted sample exceeded the threshold value for that index. In other words, more than two-thirds of College A's graduates showed a strong inclination to exhibit that particular attribute. A yellow bar (shown here as white) indicates that at least half, but not more than two-thirds, of the weighted sample exceeded the threshold value. When less than half of the respondents exceeded the threshold a blue bar (shown here as gray) is displayed. The whiskers at the end of each horizontal bar mark 95 percent confidence intervals.

College A can glean from this graph that a majority of its graduates were strongly inclined toward engaging in civic and community activities, maintaining physical fitness, and pursuing lives that included substantial involvement with Arts and Culture. On the other hand College A graduates were not likely to become engaged in religious activities: less than 15 percent exceeded the threshold for this category.

Figure 5.1 also shows that a majority of College A graduates felt they were prepared to perform tasks in all three Abilities domain categories, with more than two out of three expressing self-confidence in tasks involving quantitative skills and the ability to find information, which together represent research and interpretive skills. For the ability to communicate and organize, 65.1 percent of the weighted sample exceeded the threshold, just missing the 66.7 percent mark necessary for a red score in this index. Even then, the confidence interval for this measure—that is, the band we are 95 percent certain contains the true value of the index—stretches well above that marker.

Figure 5.1. CRI for College A

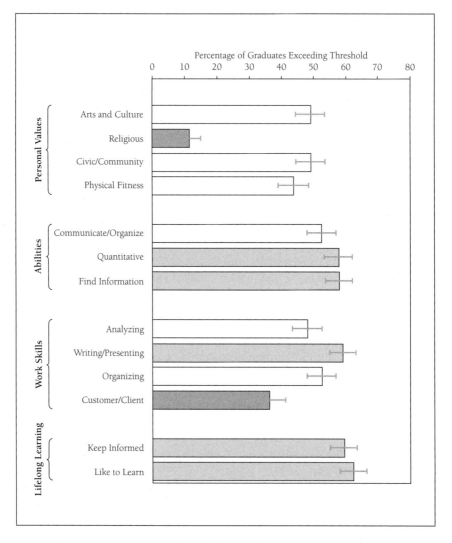

College A's graduates told a slightly different story regarding the Work Skills that they reported using on the job. Writing and presenting skills were most in demand for these alumni; exceeding the threshold at 73.4 percent, this category represented the only red bar in the set, followed by organizing skills (exceeding the threshold at 65.2 percent) and analyzing skills at 59.8 percent. Only 45.5 percent of the weighted sample consistently used customer/client skills, one of just two blue scores for College A.

Finally, more than two-thirds of College A's graduates showed a strong inclination toward keeping abreast of current events and learning more about tasks they did not yet feel fully confident to perform. They scored reds in both the keep informed and like to learn categories.

All in all, College A had a striking performance: five reds, six yellows, and two blues. Likely to bother College A's faculty were the yellow bars for the arts and culture and civic/community categories. For more than two decades much of the thrust in this liberal arts college's cocurricular activities had been in precisely this direction. The faculty might have also wondered about the low score for the customer/client category in the Work Skills domain.

Figures 5.2 through 5.4 show the results for the other three liberal arts colleges. The similarities among the four colleges reflect the basic attributes exhibited by graduates of liberal arts colleges in the last decade of the twentieth century:

- Graduates scored red for the like to learn category, indicating that more than two-thirds of their graduates said they wanted to learn about tasks they did not presently feel confident to perform.
- A clear majority of graduates kept abreast of the latest news.
- The work skill most demanded of these graduates was the need to make written or oral presentations.
- More than two-thirds of the graduates felt confident in their ability to perform tasks regarding the finding of information, which involve research and interpretive skills.
- A clear majority of graduates reported that they were strongly inclined to practice civic/community engagement.

In sum, these graduates were citizens and learners who wanted to know more about the world in which they found themselves—not a bad set of bragging rights in the increasingly competitive market for students seeking a Medallion education.

In examining the differences we found it interesting that those differences did not involve some institutions having more powerful signatures than others, if powerful is taken to mean the presence of red and the absence of blue bars. No institution had more than three or fewer than one blue bar. No institution had more than five or fewer than four red bars. The differences lay in the distribution of the three colors.

College B (see Figure 5.2), for example, is the only institution in which more than two-thirds of its graduates were likely to be strongly engaged in activities involving arts and culture. It was also the only one of the four to have less than half of its graduates report they were strongly inclined to engage in activities associated with keeping physically fit. Also potentially troubling to College B, its former students felt substantially less confident in their ability to perform quantitative tasks, scoring nine to fifteen percentage points lower than its competitors in this set of four institutions.

College C's distinctiveness (see Figure 5.3), on the other hand, lay more in the confidence of its graduates in performing tasks involving communicating and organizing. Indeed, this signature was so strong that even the lower boundary of the confidence interval (the bar's whiskers) exceeded the two-thirds mark. It is interesting to note that College C also had the highest

Figure 5.2. CRI for College B

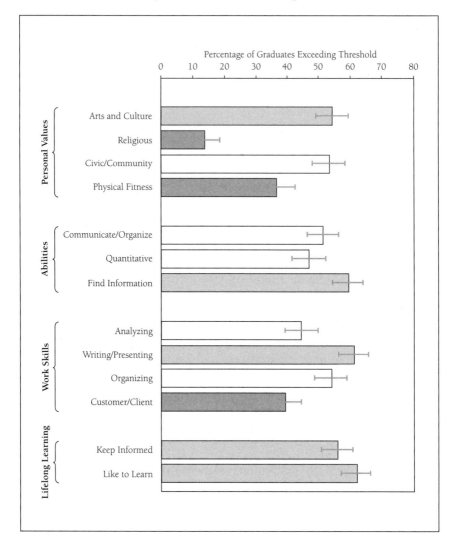

proportion of its graduates (81.3 percent) reporting that they consistently used writing and presenting skills on the job.

Finally, College D (see Figure 5.4), which generally scored higher in the rankings than the other three liberal arts colleges, might be concerned that its profile was not more distinctive: only a majority, rather than two-thirds, of its graduates were actively engaged in activities associated with arts and culture; it was one of the two institutions with yellow, as opposed to red, bars for the keep informed index; and again, a majority rather than two-thirds of its graduates felt fully confident to perform tasks involving quantitative skills. Because College D had made substantial investments

Figure 5.3. CRI for College C

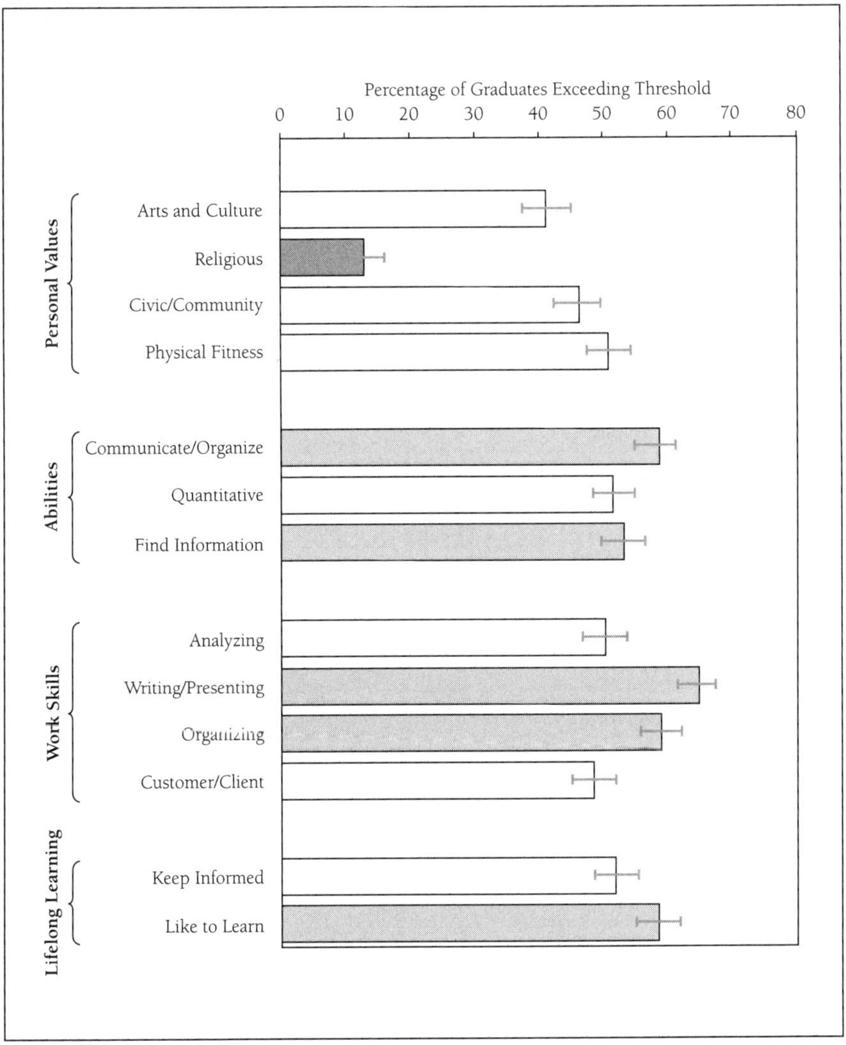

over the last decade and perhaps more in all three of these areas, the CRI results could be cause for concern.

The more pronounced—and hence more clear and understandable—differences proved to be the occupational profiles of the four colleges' recent alumni. Figure 5.5 shows the occupational distribution of the weighted sample of respondents for College A.

For the occupation graph we sorted the occupations first by color and then by percentages within the same color band (once again with black representing red, white representing yellow, and gray representing blue). Thus College A's occupational signature begins with three red bars in occupations

Figure 5.4. CRI for College D

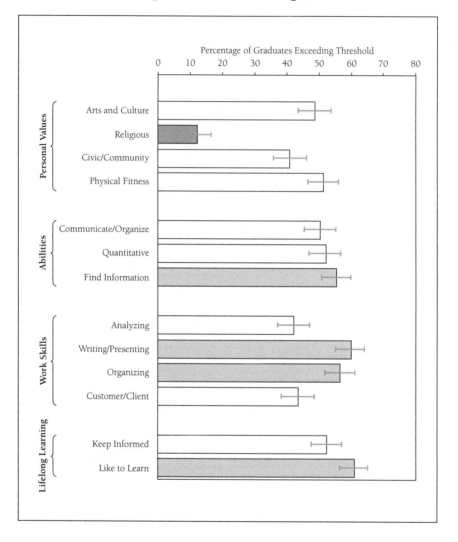

for which the percentage of College A graduates exceeded the national norm by at least 50 percent: professional (such as psychologist or librarian, but not law and medicine), law, and medicine/dentistry/veterinary. Next follow College A's two yellow bars for science/engineering/technical and teaching/counseling and finally its three blue bars for business, creative arts/design, and health/social services.

Figure 5.5 makes readily apparent the preprofessional cast of College A's recent graduates. Students attending and graduating from this college had a substantially better chance of becoming doctors and lawyers than if they had graduated from most other colleges or universities. The same held

Figure 5.5. CRI for College A, Occupations Domain

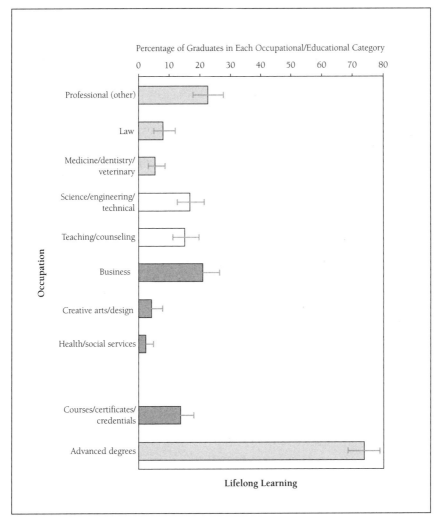

true for the other professions as well. In addition, this liberal arts college sent a significant number of its graduates into the scientific, engineering, and technical fields—an impressive achievement considering it does not have an undergraduate engineering program. The yellow score for teaching/counseling also beats the odds, given that most teachers today graduate from public as opposed to private colleges and universities.

The blue score for the business occupational category requires caution in its interpretation. In fact, the occupations within the general business category attracted the second-largest group of College A graduates (21.2 percent). College A sends large numbers of its graduates into business occupations because, quite simply, that is where the jobs are. The blue scores for creative arts/design and health/social services are genuine shortfalls indicating that those occupations hold little promise or attraction for most College A graduates.

The last two bars in Figure 5.5 report the postbaccalaureate educational experiences of College A's graduates, categories that are part of the Lifelong Learning domain but that provide a useful comparison here. As for the occupations portrayed in Figure 5.5, we normed the educational experiences against a national standard, as reflected by mean educational attainment for college graduates age twenty-seven to thirty. In College A's case comparatively few recent graduates reported taking courses or seeking additional credentials or certificates. On the other hand, three out of four College A graduates reported seeking postgraduate degrees within five years of earning their baccalaureate degrees—more than double the rate reflected in the national norm.

The push to pursue further education turns out to be a hallmark of all four Medallion liberal arts colleges in our set (see Figures 5.5, 5.6, 5.7, and 5.8). All four had red bars for advanced degrees. The other major element these institutions have in common is the proclivity to send their graduates into the professions. For all four colleges the professional (other) category topped the chart. Similarly, in all four figures both the medicine/dentistry/veterinary and law categories scored red. In much the same vein, the health/social services category was dead last on all four charts.

But once again, the differences were what fascinated us. Only College A could state that the science/engineering/technical category formed a key part of its signature. Business formed a key part of the signatures of only Colleges C and D. Only College A did not make a significant contribution to the creative arts/design occupations, whereas Colleges B and D earned red scores for this category, with College B more than doubling the national mean.

We also noted the overall shape of each of these four occupational profiles. College B faces a particular and potentially painful dilemma. Its signature has no middle ground—no yellow bars suggesting a wide range of choice. College C, on the other hand, can boast the greatest range, having a red or yellow bar in six of the eight categories.

On Making Valid Comparisons

There was, it turned out, a troubling irony in our observations. We had seen what no one else could. We alone had access to everyone's reports. We could compare College A against College D, knowing each institution's reputation as reflected in the national rankings, having access to each institution's publications, having visited each campus, and knowing and working with the leadership of each college. A number of individuals, for example, on College A's and College D's campuses know the other institution remarkably well.

Figure 5.6. CRI for College B, Occupations Domain

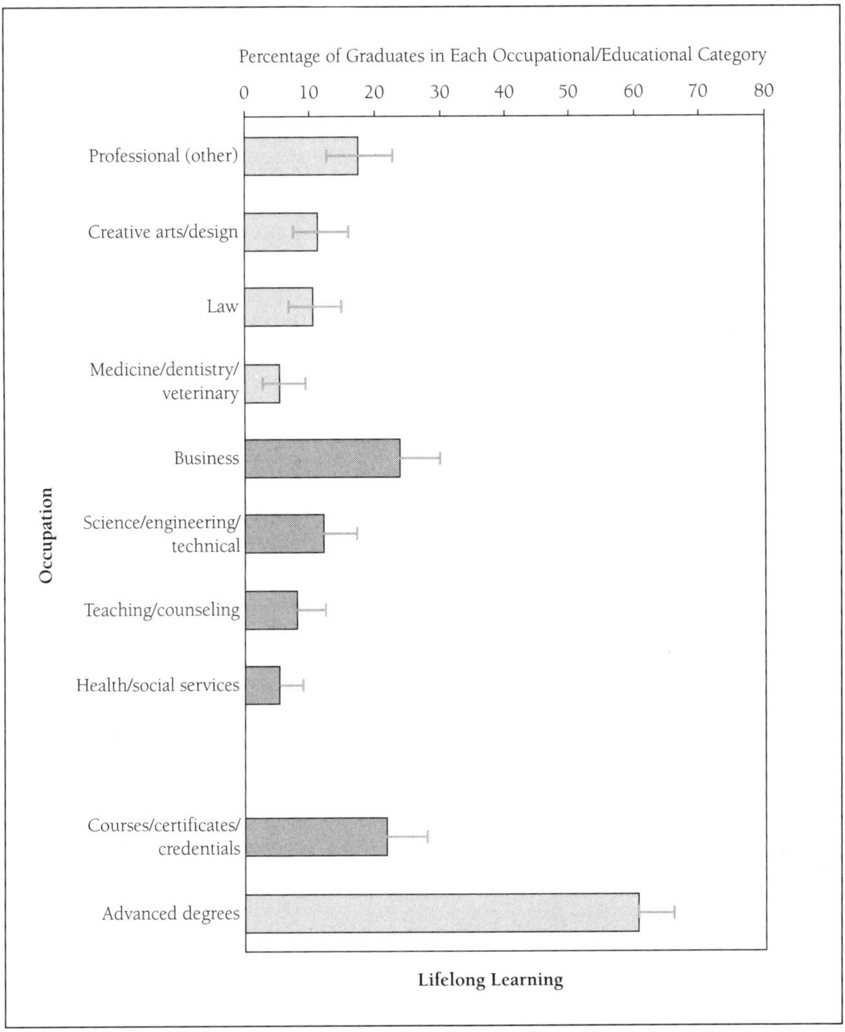

Percentage of Graduates in Each Occupational/Educational Category

What they do not know—and would like to learn without having to reveal too much about their own institution—is how the two stack up in head-to-head competition.

Much has been made of higher education's fascination with rankings. The truth is that the postsecondary enterprise loved to keep score long before *U.S. News and World Report* turned that instinct into a profitable business. As we have already mentioned, presidents routinely boast the number of Pulitzer Prize winners or Guggenheim fellows or in the case of research universities, Nobel laureates among their faculty. The number of National Merit finalists is regularly broadcast—indeed, more than one institution has

Figure 5.7. CRI for College C, Occupations Domain

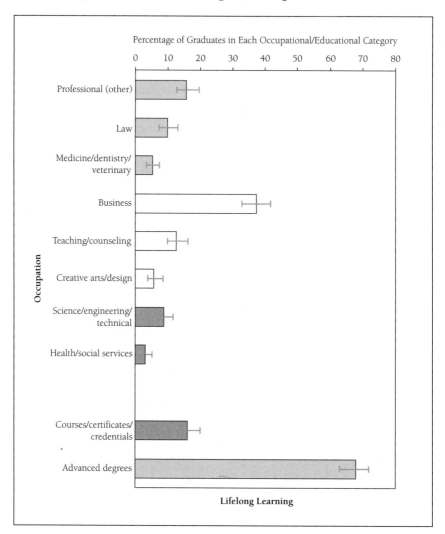

been known to invest extra scholarship funds in these finalists in order to increase their take of this valuable resource. And everybody pooh-poohs the importance of athletics, right up to the moment their team wins a national championship.

As we began distributing the CRI results, we quickly learned that most institutions wanted to know where they stood in reference to their peers—how many institutions among the eighty scored lower, and how many higher, on each of the twenty-three indices for which we reported data. We readily supplied that information, providing institutions with the number of reds, yellows, and blues that were posted for each category. We also

Figure 5.8. CRI for College D, Occupations Domain

Figure 5.8. CRI for College D, Occupations Domain

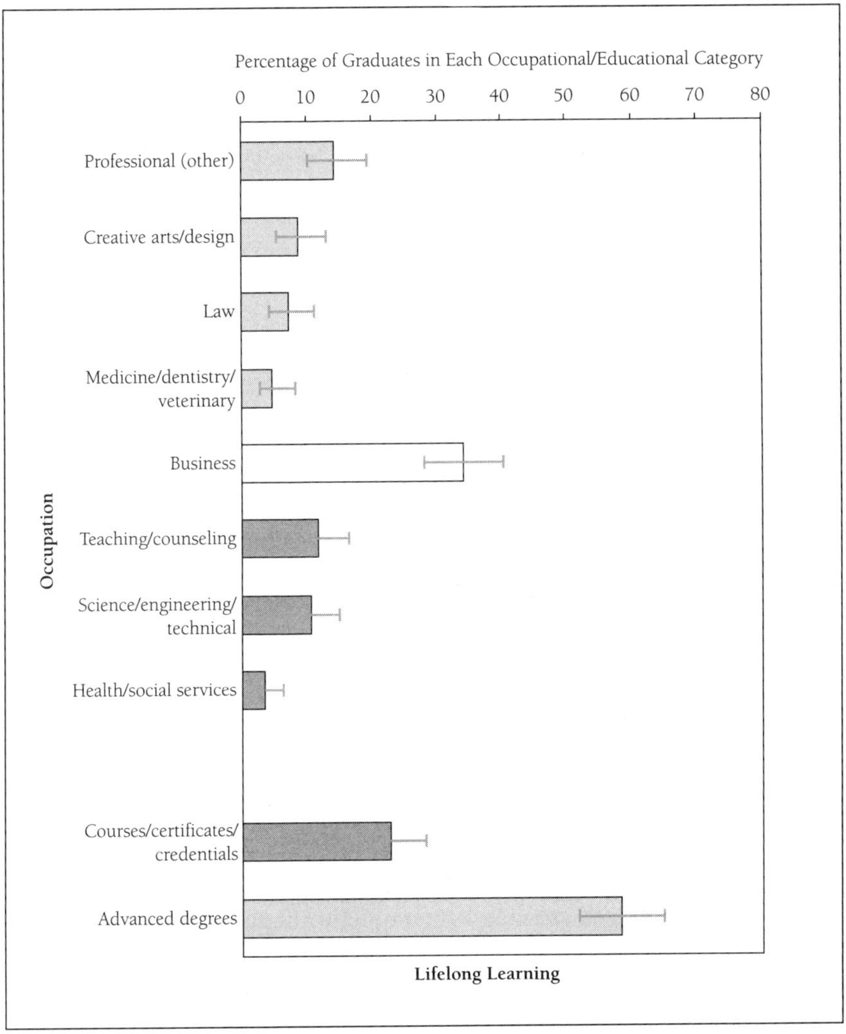

reported the same data for one of four peer groups: research universities belonging to the AAU, other research and doctoral-granting institutions, comprehensive institutions, and liberal arts colleges.

In addition, we constructed a Web-based utility that the eighty participating institutions could use to produce customized reports segmenting their own responses by a host of categories, including graduates' gender, ethnicity, major, school of enrollment, and occupation. The same Web utility allows a participating institution to pick a minimum of five institutions (using market segment and Carnegie classification) against which to compare its own profiles. Although these comparisons are useful, it became apparent that the act of aggregating data from five or more institutions had the effect of smoothing out the distinctiveness reflected in each institution's individual profile. That is what means do.

We honored in full our promise to the participating institutions not to share their data with any other institution or entity. Still, we couldn't help but ask under what conditions the institutions would readily share their profiles with each other. Under what conditions would the benefit of insight outweigh the risk of having one's competition know where an institution's profile proved less than professed?

Completing the Loop

Not surprisingly, we faced exactly the same problem of identifying institutions when we sought to complete our second task—to complete the loop by providing potential customers with the same basic information in a way that informed their choice of a college or university. Influenced no doubt by the power of the rankings, we originally planned simply to publish the profiles of sufficient numbers of colleges and universities and then let would-be customers compare those in which they were most interested. To do so, we would need not forty thousand to fifty thousand but upward of a half-million graduates to complete the CRI. Moreover, we would need to gain access to those graduates without first promising their alma maters that we would not publish the results of the CRI. Although we knew we had a reliable instrument that produced the results we were looking for, we quickly discovered that we had neither the means nor a strategy for getting the CRI in the hands of enough graduates to make the process work.

Enter Peterson's—which itself had been undergoing a substantial transformation since its acquisition by Thomson Learning, a division of Thomson Publishing of Canada. Peterson's was the granddaddy of college guides, publishing more than twenty separate guides designed to provide useful information to a growing legion of educational shoppers. Peterson's crown jewel was its *Guide to Four-Year Colleges*, a behemoth publication containing detailed sketches of more than fifteen hundred institutions arrayed across more than three thousand pages.

Peterson's new leadership understood the speed at which the Web was transforming the familiar in general and through e-commerce in particular. Peterson's new chief executive officer, Michael Brannick, asked if we would be interested in forming a partnership; he offered a means of bringing the CRI to scale by using Peterson's family of Web sites visited by recent college graduates in increasing numbers in their search for job opportunities and further schooling. He believed that enough of these graduates could be induced to fill out the CRI on-line to provide the database we sought.

Although Peterson's was not the only outlet with whom we discussed using the CRI as an aid to the college recruitment process, only Peterson's— having first guessed we had a problem—offered a potential solution. It was, it turned out, not the only thing that Peterson's offered as we sought to close the loop linking students as shoppers with colleges and universities as providers.

Peterson's first insight was that the CRI offered a unique environment in which potential students could construct their own customized rankings. Just as no institution scored a red in every category, no potential college student would be equally interested in all the dimensions the CRI tracked. Most college-bound high school juniors and seniors needed a means of sorting through their own priorities—the kinds of jobs in which they were interested, the level of educational attainment they sought, the work skills they expected to need, the abilities they thought important to develop, and the personal values they believed were important. The means Peterson's suggested for achieving that sorting was devilishly simple: the high school junior or senior needed to take the CRI—or at least a slightly amended version that tracked how the high school student wanted to turn out after college. The result would be not one but two sets of signatures: one for students and one for institutions. The task thus became a matter of determining which institutional signatures most closely resembled that student shopper's signature.

Peterson's also pointed out that in the point-and-click world of the Web, matching could not be done by simple visual inspection. No matter how pleased we might be with our graphs—and our ability to tease out the subtle differences among and between institutional signatures—most high school students would want considerably more help than that. They would want lists that made intuitive sense. We needed a search engine that, using student shoppers' own priorities, sorted and matched students and institutions.

Finally, Peterson's asked whether we could use the power of the nearly forty thousand responses to the beta round of CRI testing to build that search engine. Did we know enough about the links between an institution's public persona and the outcomes signature reflected in the lives of its recent graduates to estimate that association for institutions whose graduates had not been asked to fill out a CRI? We were not sure—indeed, we would have to convince ourselves that such a model was possible and verifiable before we could proceed.

We first needed to be sure we had a database of publicly available data about a sufficient number of institutions to make the effort worthwhile. In addition, that database would have to be sufficiently robust, including a wide range of variables reflecting institutional attributes. It turned out—not so coincidentally—that such a database did exist. We had built it as a key part of the process of developing our segmented taxonomy reflecting the structure of the market for undergraduate education. We knew the size of most institutions, their distribution of degrees by major, their location, the rate at which they converted freshmen to graduates, their admit and yield rates, their price, and the gender and ethnic distributions of their students.

Our next step was to estimate a set of regression models—twenty-three in all, one for each CRI target category—to determine if we could use the public data set to predict the CRI scores for the institutions for which we had actual CRI data. To say we were surprised by the result would be an understatement. We were flabbergasted! We could estimate models that explained more than half of the variance for all but one of the CRI indices. For more than half of the indices we could explain at least two-thirds of the variance; and for one index, an astonishing 95.9 percent. The model with the worst fit still explained 47.5 percent of the variance.

Perhaps we should not have been so surprised. What we confirmed and perhaps should have known all along was that the outcomes we were measuring were tied to some very old-fashioned notions about U.S. higher education: that curriculum matters, that educational momentum matters, that institutional size matters, and that on occasion, price matters, too. As an example, Figure 5.9 illustrates the same data for the eight Occupation categories that the CRI tracked.

Arranged across the top of the figure are the Occupation categories. Along the left-hand edge are the variables that were included in at least one of the equations used to estimate occupation. A plus sign in a cell indicates that the row's variable was significant at the .05 level in the equation predicting the column's occupation. This icon also signals that the sign of the parameter was positive. A minus sign indicates that the estimate had a significant negative value; a blank cell is an indication that the variable was not included in the final estimating equation.

The rows and columns in Figure 5.9 are arranged to highlight the three areas marked by the gray shading. The first such cluster consists of a set of seven rows containing independent variables and two columns indicating the law and business occupations. The cluster is an almost-classic representation of preprofessional undergraduate education. The probability of an institution producing lawyers increases with the percentage of its freshmen who complete their degrees in five years, the institution's yield rate, its proportion of humanities and social science majors, and its total size.

The business occupation equation is simpler. Graduates of larger institutions with many social science and business majors are more likely to go into business than those from smaller institutions with more of a spread of liberal arts majors. In the lower right-hand corner of the figure are a set of four independent variables and the two occupational groups that depend on science curricula. This cluster also illustrates something about the regression analysis. That the proportion of physicians, dentists, and veterinarians was negatively associated with the proportion of graduates with degrees in engineering, math, or computer science is a corrective that ensures that predominantly engineering schools were not falsely credited with producing physicians instead of engineers. (It should also be noted that the science/engineering occupation equation included the variable reflecting the percentage of an institution's baccalaureate earners who had

Figure 5.9. Independent Variables in the Occupation Regressions

	Law	Business	Teaching/ Counseling	Health/ Social Services	Professional (Other)	Creative Arts/ Design	Science/ Engineering	Medicine/Dental Veterinary
Five-year BA/BS degree rate	+		−					
Yield rate	+				−			
FTE enrollment	+	+			−		+	+
Tuition*	+				−		+	
Percentage of social sciences degrees	+	+						
Percentage of humanities degrees	+		+					
Percentage of business degrees		+						
Percentage of females			+	+	+			
Percentage of education degrees			+					
Percentage of health professional degrees					+			
Percentage of humanities plus languages degrees					+	+		
Percentage of other degrees					+			
Percentage of arts/design degrees						+		
Admit rate					−			
Degree production			+					
Percentage of physical sciences degrees							+	+
Percentage of math plus computer science degrees							+	
Percentage of engineering degrees							+	
Percentage of engineering plus math plus computer cegrees								−

*Tuition is out-of-state or in-state depending on the particular regression model.

majored in engineering rather than the more-inclusive variable representing the percent of graduates with degrees in the combined category of engineering, math, and computer science.)

The third cluster, the gray area in the middle of Figure 5.9, represents
occupations in which institutions with a greater proportion of women graduates tended to dominate: teaching/counseling, health/social services, and
professional (other). The links with the curriculum were straightforward—
institutions that graduated more education majors were more likely to produce teachers; those with more majors in the health professions were more
likely to send their graduates into those occupations. Only one occupational
category—creative arts/design—does not fit easily into one of the three clusters, although its association with size, with cost of attendance (as represented by out-of-state tuition), and with arts, foreign language, and
humanities majors makes good intuitive sense.

Remaining to be tested was the reliability and credibility of the regression analysis underlying Figure 5.9. To that end, we compared the actual
score derived from the CRI itself for the eighty institutions participating in
the project with the score estimated using public data and our set of regression models. Our intention was to determine how often the estimate was a
whole category different from the actual score—that is, how often the color
of the estimate, using the same basic rules, differed from the color assigned
by the analysis of CRI returns.

That analysis is summarized in Figure 5.10. As shown in the figure, the
actual and predicted index scores place an institution in the same color
group (red, yellow, or blue) over 80 percent of the time. In fact, the predicted scores are within five percentage points of the actual scores 80 percent of the time. In addition, in only 1 percent of all cases are the predicted
scores so far from the actual scores that the color assignment skips beyond
the adjacent group; that is, an actual blue is rarely predicted as red, or vice
versa. These larger skips occur almost exclusively in occupations such as
law and medicine, in which national norms are low and the yellow band is
narrow. In fact, although the occupations and education categories in Figure
5.10 display the weakest fit between actual and predicted color, the fit is
nevertheless on target 75 percent of the time.

Another way to look at this issue is to ask: How good is the fit for a
given institution? Using the same approach of matching the actual color
assignments with the predicted ones, we found that for 15 percent of the
institutions, the colors matched for at least twenty-one of the twenty-three
target categories; that is, more than 90 percent of the categories matched.
One institution had perfect alignment—twenty-three of twenty-three. A
third of the institutions scored nineteen or twenty matches out of twenty-
three, whereas 35 percent matched on sixteen to eighteen target categories.

Our last task was to develop an algorithm—what we called "The
Chooser"—with which to power a Web engine. It proved easier and more
straightforward than we had anticipated. We scored the student shopper's

Figure 5.10. Percentage of Predicted Target Colors
Matching Actual Target Colors

Color Codes Based on Actual Index Scores Versus Predicted Index Scores

Target Category	Percentage of Institutions in the Same Color Band	
Values	83	
Abilities	83	
Work Skills	78	
Lifelong Learning Indices	80	
All Indices	81	
Occupations	77	
Education	75	
Best Prediction	91	Values: Religion
Worst Prediction	68	Occupation: Health and Social Services

version of the CRI—now dubbed the BestCollegePicks Survey—exactly as we had scored the CRI, creating indices that folded into our five target categories: Personal Values, Abilities, Occupations, Work Skills, and Lifelong Learning. The Chooser's task was to match the resulting student profile against the set of institutional signatures.

Next, we sorted the 938 institutions for which we had complete data into ten buckets based on market segments, with separate public and private buckets for the Medallion, Name Brand, Good Buy, and Good Opportunity market segments. We did not split the User-Friendly/Convenience segment between public and private institutions. We assigned Bible colleges, seminaries, yeshivas, and all other institutions similarly coded by the Carnegie classification to a tenth bucket.

The result is a customized ranking based on the preferences of each individual student shopper, with no implication that one bucket is more appropriate or better than another. The student shopper receives up to ten lists of potential choices that reflect his or her own preferences.

We found no statistical way of verifying The Chooser's sorting algorithm—no rule of significance, no means of gauging how much variance is being explained. To compensate we ran The Chooser again and again, each time checking the resulting lists for obvious anomalies or omissions. We asked some questions: If the test involved students interested in creative arts/design occupations, did the resulting lists include institutions like Carnegie-Mellon University, Bard College, the Julliard School, and the Rhode Island School of Design? If the test involved business, were Babson College and the University of Pennsylvania with its Wharton School near the top of the list? If the test was medicine, was the list dominated by colleges and universities with established reputations for preprofessional education? And the ultimate test, did the list change substantially when the student input vector changed?

The answer to the last question was a gratifying "Yes." For each of the ten buckets different institutions were at the top of the list for each of the test student input variables. The loop had been closed. We had developed an analytic and data environment that both providers and consumers could use to sharpen their choices and adjust their strategies.

6

The lesson of this volume is simply that successful institutions will be those that learn to be both market smart and mission centered. In this chapter the authors propose a set of rules and tools to help institutional leaders and researchers achieve that goal.

Work Plans

Over the last two decades institutional researchers have evolved a richer understanding of higher education's markets. Much of that work has focused on the structure of these markets and the role that prices, discounts, and financial aid have played in determining where students enroll and the kind of research that wins financial support. As a consequence institutional researchers and leaders have shown both a greater willingness to think of colleges and universities as economic enterprises and a better understanding of the economics of higher education. More recently, we have seen a renewed interest in the determinants of quality and the role that systems, incentives, and cultures play in shaping higher education's response to market pressures. With the development of two broadly defined, well-financed efforts to design and test a reliable set of outcome measures, most of the basic tools needed to understand when and how markets matter are now in hand.

Researchers associated with the NCPI have undertaken a large share of this work. Often drawing on parallel experiences in the United Kingdom and Hong Kong, William Massy of Stanford University has produced the first systematic analysis of when, where, and how general programs of quality assurance can work for higher education. In partnership with Massy, we have developed an analytic strategy for identifying the margins individual institutions and enterprises earn when they provide educational services. Here, the argument is less about costs and more about the relationship between markets, prices, and margins. Massy has also extended these efforts in pursuit of an activity-based cost accounting system. Patricia Gumport, NCPI's executive director, is completing a major study of how market pressures along with calls for greater public accountability and concerns about declining public appropriations are reshaping the economies of some of this country's most important public universities. Working with Tom Bailey of Columbia University, she is also exploring the increasingly important competition between for-profit providers of postsecondary education and local community colleges.

In her role as NCPI executive director, Gumport has continually reminded us that despite higher education's current fascination with markets, colleges and universities are not businesses. We have taken her words to heart and in our own efforts have come to focus on precisely how institutions are and are not like the businesses they increasingly encounter in the marketplace. With Massy's help, we have boiled down our findings to a simple set of aphorisms that apply this focus:

- Despite public denials to the contrary, each college and university does have a bottom line. Like every entity that earns its keep by producing and selling products at competitive prices, the academy must make certain that what it sells costs less to produce than the price the public is prepared to pay for that product.
- Distinguishing a college or university from its for-profit competitors is the fact that postsecondary institutions are value centered, whereas businesses are profit centered. Put differently, colleges and universities retain their margins, choosing to invest them in things the market will not support or in ventures that promise future returns. Businesses similarly reinvest a portion of the margins they earn but distribute the rest to their stockholders as profits.
- The successful college or university must be both market smart and mission centered. The activities in which it engages therefore need to satisfy two conditions: first, most of these activities must both earn their keep and return a significant margin to support the corporate and academic goals of the institution; second, these activities must be part and parcel of the institution's sense of itself—its definition of what is important and why. The first condition captures what we mean by the phrase "market smart"; the latter, what we mean by "mission centered." We complete the syllogism by noting that an institution will earn the lion's share of the funds it needs to be mission centered by being market smart.
- Successful businesses also worry about the same issues, although they invert the syllogism: success means being market centered and mission smart. As our NCPI colleague Ann Duffield has noted, today's most successful for-profit enterprises understand that they need to be focused on the one hand and empowering on the other. It is that sense of customer empowerment in a consumer-driven economy that is increasingly separating the successful from the marginal enterprise. This axiom represents the next set of lessons from the world of business that colleges and universities will need to absorb.

We have concentrated in this volume on helping institutions understand how to be market smart. Essentially, we have argued for a more-nuanced as well as more-formal understanding of the questions and analyses that institutions ought to ask in pursuit of effective market strategies. In our estimation the following maxims summarize this approach:

- *Know your market.* Know its structure and your place in it.
- *Know what you can and cannot change.* It is easier to improve your competitive position within your market segment than try to shift to a new, presumably more competitive one.
- *Focus on retention.* It is the one strategy most likely to improve your competitive position, unless your institution really is one of its market's best-kept secrets.
- *Price accordingly.* Underpricing simply means you will have less money to invest in your educational products than your competitors, whereas over-pricing puts you at risk.
- *Understand that in consumer-driven economies, outcome measures take on added importance.* They are what the consumer wants and as a result, what the media pays attention to.
- *Use outcome measures both to improve the quality of your own products and to educate your potential customers.* When customers are badly informed, they find the kinds of products and providers they deserve.
- *Invest in institutional transparency.* Everyone, and particularly those most responsible for delivering your educational services, needs to know the market on the one hand and how your collective products measure up on the other.

In developing these recommendations, as in all of our work, we have been concerned as much with the practical as with the conceptual. Hence our rules, taken either singularly or collectively, call for specific actions designed to make an institution more enterprising, principally by making it better informed.

In this volume we have presented our work as a conceptual narrative, explaining the why and how of our efforts to make market behavior more comprehensible and therefore rational. We could have just as easily drawn on our experiences as institutional researchers and planners to provide a set of practical templates. But we believe the result would not have been sub-stantially different because our concepts derive from the practical measures and analyses we have performed for over twenty years in support of insti-tutional missions. In this guise our work offers a set of practical steps every institutional researcher and planner can—and we believe ought to—take:

- *Revenue.* The first task is to understand institutional revenues in constant dollars. The best data available are those posted on the National Science Foundation's CASPAR Web site (http://caspar.nsf.gov/). These data rep-resent what your institution submitted, prior to 1986, to the National Center for Education Statistics (NCES) through HEGIS and after 1986 to IPEDS. The key measure you should track is core revenues in constant dollars. You should ask two questions: Have my institution's core revenues enjoyed real growth over the last twenty-five years? And has the proportion of core revenues derived from tuition and fees increased, decreased, or remained about the same?

- *Segments.* Next, you will want to know your institution's market segment and determine if you are charging the right prices for your market. Here, the question you should ask is whether the actual calculated price your institution charges is in line with its market position. If your institution's actual calculated price is substantially lower than the estimated or expected value, you may be giving up revenue. If the reverse is true—if the actual calculated price is substantially higher than the estimated value—then your institution runs the risk of being overpriced.

- *Contours.* You also may want to know how different your institution is from other campuses in your own or in neighboring market segments. Although every comparison is potentially interesting, two have particular import: (1) How extensive is your institution's use of part-time faculty? (2) How diverse is your institution's student body? Here, the advantage is that the comparison is being drawn not against national averages but against the profiles of institutions that are very much like your own.

- *Results/Choices.* As we have tried to make clear, we believe an understanding of outcomes is fundamental to providing the kind of quality assurance the market is demanding. We strongly recommend that every institution participate in the two major outcomes projects now completing their development. The NSSE is administered by Indiana University and focuses on the kinds of processes and experiences seniors report as they complete their baccalaureate education. Information for the NSSE can be found at www.indiana.edu/~nsse/. The CRI is now being administered by Peterson's and has been renamed the Collegiate Results Survey (CRS). Information about the CRS and its focus on the experiences of graduates five to six years after leaving their institutions can be found at www.petersons.com. Both the NSSE and the CRS provide important opportunities for comparing the experiences of students at your institution with those of students at either similar or dissimilar institutions. Again, you should ask two key questions: Is the resulting institutional profile what we want for our institution? And if we want to make changes, what do we have to do to achieve a different kind of profile?

We close with a final observation. When markets matter, good analysis—what most colleges and universities would call institutional research and most businesses would label market research—becomes a prerequisite to success. Although intuition is always important in any strategic enterprise, what more often than not distinguishes market leaders from the rest is their tactical understanding of where their intuitions are likely to take them. It is a world in which the analysts are as important as the sales force. Good luck.

APPENDIX

THE TARGET CATEGORIES OF THE FIVE DOMAINS

Domain	Target Category
Personal values (1–4)	Arts and culture
	Religious
	Civic/community
	Physical fitness
Abilities (5–7)	Communicate/organize
	Quantitative
	Find information
Occupations (8–16)	Health/social services
	Creative arts/design
	Science/engineering/technical
	Medicine/dentistry/veterinary
	Law
	Business
	Teaching/counseling
	Professional (other)
	Nonprofessional*
Work skills (17–20)	Analyzing
	Writing/presenting
	Organizing
	Customer/client
Lifelong learning (21–24)	Keep informed
	Like to learn
	Courses/certificates/credentials
	Advanced degrees

*The category "Nonprofessional" was not included in the analysis because it comprises a collection of occupations the Bureau of Labor Statistics believes is not associated with a college degree.

Personal Values	Target Items Included in Index
Arts and culture	Question 8: b Question 9: h, i, k, m
Religious	Question 8: i Question 9: e, g
Civic/community	Question 8: c, f, h Question 9: b, r
Physical fitness	Question 8: g, j Question 9: a, l
Abilities	*Target Items Included in Index*
Communicate/organize	Scenarios a, d, e, h
Quantitative	Scenarios b, f, i
Find information	Scenarios c, g, j
Work Skills	*Target Items Included in Index*
Analyzing	Question 4: g, h, i, j, p
Writing/presenting	Question 4: d, f, n, s
Organizing	Question 4: b, c, e, l, m
Customer/client	Question 4: k, o, r, q
Lifelong Learning	*Target Items Included in Index*
Keep informed	Question 8: c, l Question 9: n, o, p, q
Like to learn	Question 11, Part 2: Responded "like to learn" to at least 1 item for which the respondent rates ability below 5, "Very well prepared"
Advanced degrees	Question 2
Courses/certificates/credentials	Question 2

CRI Occupation	CRI Table A Codes
Health/social services	29, 33
Creative arts/design	21, 38
Science/engineering/technical	22, 23, 25–27, 31, 34, 37
Medicine/dentistry/veterinary	32
Law	24
Business	11, 12, 42–44, 46, 47, 49
Teachers/counselors	35
Professional (other)	28, 36, 39
Nonprofessional	41, 45, 51–59, 61–99

REFERENCES

Chodorow, S. "The Business of Universities: Foundations for the Relationship Between the University and Industry." Paper presented at the All-University of California Conference on the Relationship Between Universities and Industry, California, 1997.

Finn, C. E. "Today's Academic Market Requires a New Taxonomy of Colleges." *Chronicle of Higher Education*, 1998, *44*(18), B4.

Institute for Research on Higher Education. "The User-Friendly Terrain: Defining the Market Taxonomy for Two-Year Institutions." *Change*, 1998, *30*(1), 57–60.

Peterson's. *Peterson's Guide to Four-Year Colleges*. Princeton, N.J.: Peterson's, 1999.

Policy Perspectives, 2(4), June 1990.

Shaman, S., and Zemsky, R. "Perspectives on Pricing." In L. H. Litten (ed.), *Issues in Pricing Undergraduate Education*. New Directions for Institutional Research, no. 42. San Francisco: Jossey-Bass, 1984.

Woodward, C. "Worldwide Tuition Increases Send Students into the Streets." *Chronicle of Higher Education*, 2000, *46*(35), A54.

Zemsky, R., and Oedel, P. *The Structure of College Choice*. Princeton, N.J.: College Board, 1983.

Zemsky, R., and Massy, W. F. "Expanding Perimeters, Melting Cores, and Sticky Functions: Toward an Understanding of Our Current Predicaments." *Change*, 1995, *27*(6), 41–49.

Zemsky, R., Massy, W., and Oedel, P. "On Reversing the Ratchet." *Change*, 1993, *25*(3), 56–62.

Zemsky, R., Shaman, S., and Iannozzi, M. "In Search of Strategic Perspective: A Tool for Mapping the Market in Postsecondary Education." *Change*, 1997, *29*(6), 23–38.

Other Resources

Ahn, T., Charnes, A., and Cooper, W. "DEA and Ratio Efficiency Analysis for Public Institutions of Higher Learning in Texas." In J. L. Chan (ed.), *Research in Government and Non-Profit Accounting*. Greenwich, Conn.: JAI Press, 1989.

Beasley, J. E. "Determining Teaching and Research Efficiencies." *Journal of the Operations Research Society*, 1995, *46*, 441–452.

Besanko, D., Dranove, D., and Shanley, M. *The Economics of Strategy*. New York: Wiley, 1996.

Bowen, H. *The Costs of Higher Education*. San Francisco: Jossey-Bass, 1980.

Clotfelter, C. T. *Buying the Best: Cost Escalation in Elite Higher Education*. Princeton, N.J.: Princeton University Press, 1996.

Ganley, J. A., and Cubbin, J. S. *Public Sector Efficiency: Applications of Data Envelopment Analysis*. Amsterdam: North Holland, 1992.

Hansmann, H. "Higher Education as an Associative Good." Paper presented at the Symposium of the Forum for the Future of Higher Education. Aspen, Colorado, September 1998.

Hopkins, D., and Massy, W. F. *Planning Models for Colleges and Universities*. Stanford, Calif.: Stanford University Press, 1981.

Institute for Research on Higher Education. "The Heart of the Matter: What Really Drives the Cost of an Undergraduate Education?" *Change*, 1997, *29*(4), 47–50.

James, E. "How Nonprofits Grow: A Model." *Journal of Policy Analysis*, 1982, *2*, 350–366.

James, E. "Decision Processes and Priorities in Higher Education." In S. A. Hoenack and E. L. Collins (eds.), *The Economics of American Universities*. Albany, N.Y.: SUNY Press, 1990.

James, E., and Neuberger, E. "The University Department as a Non-Profit Labor Cooperative." *Public Choice*, 1981, *36*, 585–612.

Johnston, J. S., Shaman, S., and Zemsky, R. *Unfinished Design: The Humanities and Social Sciences in Undergraduate Engineering Education.* Washington, D.C.: Association of American Colleges, 1988.

Larson, E. "Why Colleges Cost Too Much." *Time*, 1997, *149*(11). http://www.time.com/time/magazine/archives/

Litten, L. H. (ed.). *Issues in Pricing Undergraduate Education.* New Directions for Institutional Research, no. 42. San Francisco: Jossey-Bass, 1984.

Massy, W. F. *Resource Allocation in Higher Education.* Ann Arbor: University of Michigan Press, 1996.

Massy, W. F., and Zemsky, R. *Using Information Technology to Enhance Academic Productivity.* Washington, D.C.: Educom, 1995.

Stringfield, S. "Attempting to Enhance Students' Learning Through Innovative Programs." *School Effectiveness and School Improvement*, 1995, *6*, 62–96.

Tomkins, C., and Green, R. "An Experimental Use of Data Envelopment Analysis in Evaluating the Efficiency of UK Departments of Accounting." *Financial Accountability and Management*, 1988, *4*, 147–164.

Varian, H. R. *Computational Economics and Finance.* New York: Springer-Verlag, 1996.

Zemsky, R. *Structure and Coherence: Measuring the Undergraduate Curriculum.* Washington, D.C.: Association of American Colleges, 1989.

INDEX

Back Issue/Subscription Order Form

Copy or detach and send to:
Jossey-Bass, 350 Sansome Street, San Francisco CA 94104-1342

Call or fax toll free!
Phone 888-378-2537 6AM-5PM PST; Fax 800-605-2665

Back issues: Please send me the following issues at $27 each:
(Important: please include series initials and issue number, such as IR90)

1. IR _____

_____

_____

$ _____ Total for single issues

$ _____ Shipping charges (for single issues *only;* subscriptions are exempt from shipping charges): Up to $30, add $5^{50} • $30^{01}–$50, add $6^{50} $50^{01}–$75, add $8 • $75^{01}–$100, add $10, $100^{01}–$150, add $12 Over $150, call for shipping charge

Subscriptions Please ❏ start ❏ renew my subscription to *New Directions for Institutional Research* for the year _____ at the following rate:

U.S.	❏ Individual $59	❏ Institutional $109
Canada:	❏ Individual $59	❏ Institutional $154
All Others:	❏ Individual $83	❏ Institutional $183

$ _____ Total single issues and subscriptions (Add appropriate sales tax for your state for single issue orders. No sales tax for U.S. subscriptions. Canadian residents, add GST for subscriptions and single issues.)

❏ Payment enclosed (U.S. check or money order only)
❏ VISA, MC, AmEx, Discover Card #_____ Exp. date_____

Signature _____ Day phone _____
❏ Bill me (U.S. institutional orders only. Purchase order required)
Purchase order #_____
Federal Tax ID 135593032   GST 89102-8052

Name _____
Address _____

_____

Phone_____ E-mail _____

For more information about Jossey-Bass, visit our Web site at:
www.josseybass.com   **PRIORITY CODE = ND1**